THE PODCAST BOOK
2017

ORLANDO RIOS

PODCASTING PRO

The Podcast Book
2017

Copyright © 2017 by Orlando Rios Publishing

ISBN-13: 978-0692822784
ISBN-10: 069282278X

Podcasting Pro
www.podcastingpro.com
info@podcastingpro.com

Follow:

@orlandorios
@podcastingpro

/orlandoriospage
/podcastingpro

Printed in U.S.A

CONTENTS

WELCOME TO THE PODCAST BOOK

In just the last year, podcast consumption grew by over 20 percent. That equates to about 57 million total podcast listeners in the United States alone. With such growth in the popularity of podcasts from listeners, it stands to reason that there would be a growth in the total number of podcasts available overall too.

If you took one look into your iTunes podcast charts and did a deep scroll, you would see an endless amount of podcasts to choose from. While the variety is a luxury, finding a new show to listen to can be quite overwhelming.

This is why I created *The Podcast Book*.

As I found myself trying to scroll and click back-and-forth through hundreds of podcast descriptions, I found it hard to find something new to listen to. It was like searching for a needle in a haystack.

What is the best podcast in a certain category, how long is each episode, how often do new episodes come out, and who are the hosts? These are all questions that I found myself asking when looking for my next favorite show for my daily commute.

With this new book, I hope to make your search a little easier. Using all the latest top chart data, I've put together listings for every category available in iTunes in a simple and easy-to-read format. I also included the host, run time, and frequency information when it was available.

Finding a new podcast can offer a wealth of education and entertainment, so read through your favorite categories, take a highlighter, and mark the listings that interest you most.

Enjoy the hunt,
Orlando Rios

ARTS

2017 Arts Top Pick
FRESH AIR
Host: Terry Gross
Frequency: Daily
Average Show Length:
50 Minutes

Fresh Air from WHYY, the Peabody Award-winning weekday magazine of contemporary arts and issues, is one of public radio's most popular programs. Hosted by Terry Gross, the show features intimate conversations with today's biggest luminaries.

The Moth
Narrator: Various
Frequency: Weekly
Average Show Length:
50 Minutes

Description:
Since its launch in 1997, The Moth has presented thousands of true stories, told live and without notes, to standing-room-only crowds worldwide. Moth storytellers stand alone, under a spotlight, with only a microphone and a roomful of strangers. The storyteller and the audience embark on a high-wire act of shared experience which is both terrifying and exhilarating. Since 2008, The Moth podcast has featured many of our favorite stories told live on Moth stages around the country.

The No Sleep Podcast
Host: David Cummings
Frequency: Daily
Average Show Length: 60 Minutes

Description:
The NoSleep Podcast is a multi-award winning anthology series of original horror stories, with rich atmospheric music to enhance the frightening tales.

99% Invisible
Host: Roman Mars
Frequency: Daily
Average Show Length: 30 Minutes

Description:
Design is everywhere in our lives, perhaps most importantly in the places where we've just stopped noticing. 99% Invisible is a weekly exploration of the process and power of design and architecture. From award winning producer Roman Mars.

The Cleansed
Writer: Frederick Greenhalgh
Frequency: Daily
Average Show Length: 60 Minutes

Description:
Equal parts "Mad Max" and "The Stand," this post apocalyptic saga is set in a world 15 years after the collapse of the world as we know it. A brother and sister grow up in rural Maine and unwittingly embark on a adventure to save the City from the religious zealots and ruthless military fight for control over the fallen world. An epic serialized audio drama adventure with 30+ actors, cinematic sound design and original music. Winner of Mark Time Award for sci-fi audio and finalist in Romania's Grand Prix Nova award.

The Black Tapes
Host: Alex Reagan
Frequency: BiWeekly
Average Show Length: 40 Minutes

Description:
The Black Tapes is a weekly podcast from the creators of Pacific Northwest Stories, and is hosted by Alex Reagan. The Black Tapes Podcast is a serialized docudrama about one journalist's search for truth, her subject's mysterious past, and the literal and figurative ghosts that haunt them both. Do you believe?

Snap Judgement
Host: Glynn Washington
Frequency: Weekly
Average Show Length: 50 Minutes

Description:
Snap Judgment (Storytelling, with a BEAT) mixes real stories with killer beats to produce cinematic, dramatic, kick-ass radio. Snap's raw, musical brand of storytelling dares listeners to see the world through the eyes of another. WNYC studios is the producer of leading podcasts including Radiolab, Freakonomics Radio, Note To Self, Here's The Thing With Alec Baldwin, and more.

Tanis
Host: Nic Silver
Frequency: BiWeekly
Average Show Length: 40 Minutes

Description:
Tanis is a bi-weekly podcast from the creators of Pacific Northwest Stories, and is hosted by Nic Silver. Tanis is a serialized docudrama about a fascinating and surprising mystery: the myth of Tanis. Tanis is an exploration of the nature of truth, conspiracy, and information. Tanis is what happens when the lines of science and fiction start to blur.

The Sporkful
Host: Dan Pashman
Frequency: Weekly
Average Show Length: 30 Minutes

Description:
We obsess about food to learn more about people. The Sporkful isn't for foodies, it's for eaters. Hosted by Dan Pashman from Cooking Channel's You're Eating It Wrong and the book Eat More Better. New episodes on Tuesdays, bonus shows whenever we can. WNYC Studios is the producer of other leading podcasts including Radiolab, Death, Sex & Money, Freakonomics Radio and many others.

Secret Crimes & Audiotape
Host: David Rheinstrom
Frequency: Weekly
Average Show Length: 30 Minutes

Description:
An audio drama told week after week. We will bring you stories about crime, love, mystery and conspiracy. Some will make you laugh. Some will make you think. All will make you wonder... What's your secret?

Alice Isn't Dead
Writer: Joseph Fink
Frequency: BiWeekly
Average Show Length: 30 Minutes

Description:
A new fiction serial from the creator of Welcome to Night Vale, Alice Isn't Dead follows a truck driver in her search across America for the wife she had long assumed was dead. In the course of her search, she will encounter not-quite-human serial murderers, towns literally lost in time, and a conspiracy that goes way beyond one missing woman. Performed by Jasika Nicole. Written by Joseph Fink. Produced by Disparition. Part of the Night Vale Presents network.

Magic Lessons with Elizabeth Gilbert
Host: Elizabeth Gilbert
Frequency: Weekly
Average Show Length: 60 Minutes

Description:
Bestselling author Elizabeth Gilbert returns for the second season of her hit podcast MAGIC LESSONS, ready to help another batch of aspiring artists overcome their fears and create more joyfully. This year's guest experts include Neil Gaiman, Gary Shteyngart, Amy Purdy, Michael Ian Black, Brandon Stanton, Martha Beck, and Glennon Doyle Melton.

The Deep Vault
Writer: Marc Sollinger
Frequency: BiWeekly
Average Show Length: 30 Minutes

Description:
From the creators of Archive 81 comes The Deep Vault, a serialized audio drama set in an almost-post-apocalyptic United States. The story follows a group of longtime friends as they journey from the uninhabitable surface world into a mysterious underground bunker in search of safety and shelter.

The Bright Sessions
Writer: Lauren Shippen
Frequency: Weekly
Average Show Length: 30 Minutes

Description:
Dr. Bright provides therapy for the strange and unusual; their sessions have been recorded for research purposes.

Young House Love Has A Podcast
Hosts: Sherry & John Petersik
Frequency: Weekly
Average Show Length: 30 Minutes

Description:
Deep (and not-so-deep) conversations about home improvement, design, and life at home. Tune in for weekly episodes filled with casual decorating advice, DIY stories, and a smattering of home related games, along with what's new around the house and interviews with designers, bloggers, TV personalities, and more. Sherry and John Petersik are the married duo who began chronicling their home improvement adventures in 2007 on the blog Young House Love, which spawned two New York Times best-selling books, as well as product lines sold by Target and Home Depot. And, well, now they have a podcast.

Risk!
Host: Kevin Allison
Frequency: Weekly
Average Show Length: 60 Minutes

Description:
If you like The Moth, This American Life or Snap Judgment, take a walk on the wilder side with RISK! Your colorful host Kevin Allison (of the legendary comedy group The State) helms this surprisingly uncensored show where people tell jaw-dropping true stories they never thought they'd dare to share in public. RISK! is hilarious, heart-wrenching and remarkably real. Think you've heard it all? Fasten your seatbelt.

The Truth
Writer: Jonathan Mitchell
Frequency: Monthly
Average Show Length: 30 Minutes

Description:
THE TRUTH makes movies for your ears. They're short stories that are sometimes dark, sometimes funny, and always intriguing. Every story is different, but they all take you to unexpected places using only sound. If you're new, some good starting places are: Silvia's Blood, That's Democracy, Moon Graffiti, Tape Delay, or whatever's most recent. Listening with headphones is encouraged! We're a proud member of Radiotopia from PRX.

The Splendid Table
Host: Lynne Rossetto
Frequency: Weekly
Average Show Length: 50 Minutes

Description:
American Public Media's The Splendid Table is public radio's culinary, culture, and lifestyle program that celebrates food and its ability to touch the lives and feed the souls of everyone. Each week, award-winning host Lynne Rossetto Kasper leads listeners on a journey of the senses and hosts discussions with a variety of writers and personalities who share their passion for the culinary delights.

America's Test Kitchen Radio
Host: Chris Kimball
Frequency: Weekly
Average Show Length: 50 Minutes

Description:
America's Test Kitchen is a real 2,500 square foot test kitchen located just outside of Boston that is home to more than three-dozen full-time cooks and product testers. Our mission is simple: to develop the absolute best recipes for all of your favorite foods. To do this, we test each recipe 30, 40, sometimes as many as 70 times, until we arrive at the combination of ingredients, technique, temperature, cooking time, and equipment that yields the best, most-foolproof recipe.

Crime Writers On...
Host: Rebecca Lavoie and Kevin Flynn
Frequency: Weekly
Average Show Length: 80 Minutes

Description:
True crime authors and real-life couple Rebecca Lavoie and Kevin Flynn hold a pop-culture roundtable with noir novelist Toby Ball and journalist-turned-investigator Lara Bricker. The panel chats about the blockbuster podcast 'Serial,' as well as journalism, storytelling, TV shows and films, and the special segment, 'Crime of the Week.' This podcast is AKA Crime Writers On...Serial (& More!)

Imaginary Worlds
Host: Eric Molinsky
Frequency: BiWeekly
Average Show Length: 20 Minutes

Description:
Imaginary Worlds is a bi-weekly podcast about science fiction and other fantasy genres -- how we create them and why we suspend our disbelief. These are the backstories to our stories.

Tangentially Speaking
Host: Dr. Christopher Ryan
Frequency: BiWeekly
Average Show Length: 120 Minutes

Description:
Ever wanted to hang with a comedian, dominatrix, health guru, bank robber, author, or Italian prince? Well, here's your chance. Tangentially Speaking is dedicated to the idea that good conversation is organic, uncensored, revelatory, and free to go down unexpected paths.

Inside the New York Times Book Reviews
Host: Pamela Paul
Frequency: Weekly
Average Show Length: 50 Minutes

Description:
The world's top authors and critics join host Pamela Paul and editors at The New York Times Book Review to talk about the week's top books, what we're reading and what's going on in the literary world.

Gastropod
Hosts: Cynthia Graber and Nicola Twilley
Frequency: BiWeekly
Average Show Length: 50 Minutes

Description:
Food with a side of science and history. Every other week, co-hosts Cynthia Graber and Nicola Twilley serve up a brand new episode exploring the hidden history and surprising science behind a different food- or farming-related topic, from aquaculture to ancient feasts, from cutlery to chile peppers, and from microbes to Malbec. We interview experts, visit labs, fields, and archaeological digs, and generally have lots of fun while discovering new ways to think about and understand the world through food.

BUSINESS

2017 Business Top Pick
HOW I BUILT THIS
Host: Guy Raz
Frequency: Weekly
Average Show Length:
40 Minutes

How I Built This is a podcast about innovators, entrepreneurs, and idealists, and the stories behind the movements they built. Each episode is a narrative journey marked by triumphs, failures, serendipity and insight — told by the founders of some of the world's best known companies and brands.

Easy Residual Income
Host: Mike Gazzola
Frequency: Weekly
Average Show Length: 30 Minutes

Description:
Learn how to make a six figure income or more selling on Amazon. It's easy to do if you know the right steps to take. In less than 7 months we sold over $300,000 netting $150,000. We show you how to do it from the comfort of your own home with a step by step approach that will help you succeed. You'll learn from two long time successful internet marketers who've sold millions over the internet.

Planet Money
Host: Various
Frequency: Daily
Average Show Length: 30 Minutes

Description:
The economy, explained, with stories and surprises. Imagine you could call up a friend and say, "Meet me at the bar and tell me what's going on with the economy." Now imagine that's actually a fun evening. That's what we're going for at Planet Money. People seem to like it.

The Tim Ferriss Show
Host: Tim Ferriss
Frequency: Weekly
Average Show Length: 120 Minutes

Description:
Tim Ferriss is a self-experimenter and bestselling author, best known for
The 4-Hour Workweek, which has been translated into 40+ languages.
Newsweek calls him "the world's best human guinea pig," and The New
York Times calls him "a cross between Jack Welch and a Buddhist monk."
In this show, he deconstructs world-class performers from eclectic areas
(investing, chess, pro sports, etc.), digging deep to find the tools, tactics,
and tricks that listeners can use.

The Dave Ramsey Show
Host: Dave Ramsey
Frequency: Daily
Average Show Length: 40 Minutes

Description:
The Dave Ramsey Show is about real life and how it revolves around
money. Dave Ramsey teaches you to manage and budget your money, get
out of debt, build wealth, and live in financial peace. Managing your money
properly will reduce stress, improve your marriage, and provide security for
you and your family.

StartUp Podcast
Host: Alex Blumberg
Frequency: Weekly
Average Show Length: 30 Minutes

Description:
A series about what it's really like to start a business.

The Lance Tamashiro Show
Host: Lance Tamashiro
Frequency: Daily
Average Show Length: 30 Minutes

Description:
Delivering no nonsense, real and practical steps and strategies that'll have
you making money. Don't have a business? Stay tuned and grab some
ideas that'll get you taking action and not just sitting around thinking about

it. The Lance Tamashiro Show is only for you if you're a serious action-taker ready to make real money working your own business and getting real results.

The Art of Charm
Host: Jordan Harbinger
Frequency: Daily
Average Show Length: 45 Minutes

Description:
The Art of Charm Podcast is where self-motivated guys and gals, just like you, come to learn from a diverse mix of experienced mentors, including the world's best professional and academic minds, scientists, relationship experts, entrepreneurs, bestselling authors, and other badasses. This show will make you a better networker, better connector, and -- most important -- a better thinker.

Jocko Podcast
Host: Jocko Willink
Frequency: Weekly
Average Show Length: 160 Minutes

Description:
Retired Navy SEAL, Jocko Willink and Director, Echo Charles discuss discipline and ownership in business, war, relationships and everyday life.

TEDTalks Business
Host: Various
Frequency: Weekly
Average Show Length: 15 Minutes

Description:
Some of the world's greatest innovators, entrepreneurs, and business researchers share their stories and insights from the stage at TED conferences, TEDx events and partner events around the world. You can also download these and many other videos for free from TED.com that features interactive English transcript, and subtitles in as many as 80 languages. TED is a nonprofit devoted to Ideas Worth Spreading.

BiggerPockets Podcast
Hosts: Josh Dorkin and Brandon Turner
Frequency: Weekly
Average Show Length: 90 Minutes

Description:
The BiggerPockets Podcast cuts out the hype and BS, and delivers real, actionable advice from active real estate investors and other professionals in the industry. The show isn't about helping you get rich overnight or about selling you on some course, boot camp, or guru system; it is about keeping it real . . . nothing more! BiggerPockets is a free community of over 1,300,000 monthly unique visitors who are like-minded real estate enthusiasts seeking to become better real estate investors.

Sales Questions - Brutally Honest Answers
Host: Brian Burns
Frequency: Weekly
Average Show Length: 60 Minutes

Description:
You have Sales Questions and I have Ideas and some answers. You ask and I work to help.

Girlboss Radio
Host: Sophia Amoruso
Frequency: Weekly
Average Show Length: 45 Minutes

Description:
On each episode, Nasty Gal founder and author of #Girlboss Sophia Amoruso interviews world-class girlbosses who have made their mark in creative, cultural, and business ventures to extract solid advice from the lessons they've learned along the way. Expect hilarious co-hosts and conversations you won't hear anywhere else. On this podcast Sophia hopes to humanize the known, champion the unknown, and, well, laugh a little about the absurdity that is life. Are you ready?

The Brutal Truth About Sales & Selling
Host: Brian Burns
Frequency: Weekly
Average Show Length: 45 Minutes

Description:
No BS Allowed - Are you sick of empty suits telling you just work harder? - Learn about The Maverick Selling Method, models the world's best salespeople and what they do differently. If you are in sales and have a passion for selling you will like this podcast. The focus is on b2b sales and selling. If are selling or in sales this podcast is for you. Some of the topics I cover are cold calling, spin selling, challenger sale, solution selling, advanced selling skills. strategic selling, linkedin, saas, sales leadership, sales management, social media, b2b marketing, maverick selling method and how sales has changed.

EntreLeadership
Host: Ken Coleman
Frequency: Weekly
Average Show Length: 45 Minutes

Description:
Hosted by Ken Coleman, the EntreLeadership Podcast features lively discussions and tips on leadership and business by some of the top minds in the business, like Mark Cuban, Seth Godin, Jim Collins and Simon Sinek.

HBR IdeaCast
Host: Sarah Green Carmichael
Frequency: Weekly
Average Show Length: 20 Minutes

Description:
A weekly podcast featuring the leading thinkers in business and management from Harvard Business Review.

The #AskGaryVee Show
Host: Gary Vaynerchuk
Frequency: Weekly
Average Show Length: 30 Minutes

Description:
Welcome to The #AskGaryVee show, where I answer your questions about marketing, social media, and entrepreneurship.

Smart Passive Income
Host: Pat Flynn
Frequency: Weekly
Average Show Length: 60 Minutes

Description:
Pat Flynn from The Smart Passive Income Blog reveals all of his online business and blogging strategies, income sources and killer marketing tips and tricks so you can be ahead of the curve with your online business or blog. Discover how you can create multiple passive income streams that work for you so that you can have the time and freedom to do what you love, whether it's traveling the world, or just living comfortably at home.

The Dave Portnoy Show
Host: Dave Portnoy
Frequency: Weekly
Average Show Length: 60 Minutes

Description:
Introducing the Dave Portnoy Show. This show will focus on the inner workings of Barstool Sports. We'll talk about all the controversies, decisions and stories from the past that helped mold who we are today as well as questions that will define the future. Basically an in-depth look behind the curtain of one of the most controversial blogs on the planet and the guys who make it tick.

Money For The Rest of Us
Host: J. David Stein
Frequency: Weekly
Average Show Length: 30 Minutes

Description:
A personal finance show on money, how it works, how to invest it and how to live without worrying about it. J. David Stein is a former Chief Investment Strategist and money manager. For close to two decades, he has been teaching individuals and institutions how to invest and handle their finances in ways that are simple to understand.

Chris Hogan's Retire Inspired
Host: Chris Hogan
Frequency: Weekly
Average Show Length: 45 Minutes

Description:
Number-one, best-selling author Chris Hogan wants to turn the tables on how we think about retirement. Retirement isn't an age; it's a financial number! It's not about how old you are; it's about how much money you need to live your retirement dream! In each episode, America's trusted voice on retirement unpacks topics like saving, investing, budgeting, building wealth, and everything else you need to win long-term. Plus he answers your questions and highlights successful men and women who are winning the retirement game. Whether you're 25 or 55, this podcast will change your life—today and tomorrow!

EOFire
Host: John Lee Dumas
Frequency: Daily
Average Show Length: 30 Minutes

Description:
Awarded 'Best of iTunes', EOFire is a 7-day a week Podcast where John Lee Dumas chats with today's most successful Entrepreneurs. Pat Flynn, Seth Godin, Tim Ferriss, Tony Robbins and Gary Vaynerchuk are just 5 of the over 1400 interviews to date. EOFire was created for YOU, the Entrepreneur, Side-Preneur, Solo-Preneur and Small Business Owner. If you're looking for ACTIONABLE advice during your daily commute, workout, or 'me' time, JLD brings the HEAT. Each episode details the journey of a successful Entrepreneur who shares their WORST Entrepreneurial moment and lessons learned, an AH-HA moment and how they turned that idea into success, and much more. Each episode ends with THE LIGHTNING ROUND where JLD extracts golden nuggets, Internet resources and action steps for you, FIRE NATION!

We Study Billionaires
Host: Preston Psyh and Stig Brodersen
Frequency: Weekly
Average Show Length: 50 Minutes

Description:
We like to have fun and study billionaires. We interview entrepreneurs and highly influential authors of business books.

The MFCEO Project
Host: Andy Frisella
Frequency: Weekly
Average Show Length: 20 Minutes

Description:
The MFCEO Project is for anyone who is sick of the fluffy unicorns and rainbows style of talking about pursuing goals and profiting in business. In this podcast, Andy Frisella (and his guests) share insights on success and failure, in straight up fashion. An entrepreneur, innovator, motivator, and regular dude, Frisella is the founder of Supplement Superstores and 1st Phorm International, multi-million dollar companies that manufacture and sell nutritional, weight loss, and fitness products. He is motivated by a desire to help people to succeed in business and life, "to get them moving in the right direction to achieve their business and personal goals, whatever they may be."

The Ziglar Show
Hosts: Kevin Miller and Tom Ziglar
Frequency: Weekly
Average Show Length: 20 Minutes

Description:
Inspiring True Performance means truly taking action and making positive change in your life. In this show, hosts Kevin Miller and Tom Ziglar take the most powerful messages from Zig Ziglar and today's top world changers and break them down to the nitty gritty so we can all understand, digest and take real steps forward in our lives, loves, vocations and legacies. Zig Ziglar is widely recognized as the world leader in Motivation & Inspiration (the fuel for all we do!) and has reached and influenced over 250 million people through his best-selling books, legendary presentations and timeless messages. He is one of the most quoted leaders of all time.

WSJ What's News
Host: John Wordock
Frequency: Daily
Average Show Length: 10 Minutes

Description:
Stay informed of breaking news throughout your day with senior editor John Wordock of The Wall Street Journal. Listen to critical news and engaging interviews, featuring executives, economists and notable WSJ editors discuss business, markets and more.

Masters in Business
Host: Barry Ritholtz
Frequency: Weekly
Average Show Length: 60 Minutes

Description:
Bloomberg View columnist Barry Ritholtz looks at the people and ideas that shape markets, investing and business.

Exchanges at Goldman Sachs
Host: Various
Frequency: Weekly
Average Show Length: 30 Minutes

Description:
In each episode of "Exchanges at Goldman Sachs," people from the firm share their insights on developments shaping industries, markets and the global economy.

Marketplace
Host: Kai Ryssdal
Frequency: Weekly
Average Show Length: 25 Minutes

Description:
Marketplace® is the leading business news program in the nation. Host Kai Ryssdal and our team of reporters bring you clear explorations of how economic news affects you, through stories, conversations, newsworthy numbers and more. Airing each weekday evening on your local public radio station or on-demand anytime, Marketplace is your liaison between economics and life.

This Morning with Gordon Deal
Host: Gordon Deal
Frequency: Daily
Average Show Length: 30 Minutes

Description:
Wake-up with America's first news - Host Gordon Deal goes beyond the headlines with the day's first look at news and business news from the U.S. and around the world; bringing a lively blend of intelligent information, humor, and expert analysis to morning radio.

Build Your Tribe

Host: Charlene Johnson
Frequency: Weekly
Average Show Length: 30 Minutes

Description:
How to create influence that matters and content that creates conversion. Interviews and practical strategies from top internet influencers on how to build your email list, create a virtual community, strengthen a tribe and bring a powerful group of like minded people together to make a difference in the world. How to create passive income by learning best practices to cultivate, build and care for customers , community and tribe. How to serve your community with integrity and value, with tips to work less and create more.

Online Marketing Made Easy

Host: Amy Porterfield
Frequency: Weekly
Average Show Length: 40 Minutes

Description:
"Facebook Marketing All in One for Dummies" co-author and online entrepreneur Amy Porterfield shows you exactly how to monetize your online marketing and blogging efforts using her own tested, ACTIONABLE lead generation strategies -- so you can successfully launch and promote a new program, grow your email list, get more leads, build your authority, turn your customers into raving advocates OR simply find the time (and mindset!) to rock your social media and content marketing. From creating an online course to video marketing, webinar recording, Facebook, Twitter, Pinterest, YouTube, new content creation (including eBooks, guides and cheat sheets) and email marketing, Amy is going to reveal what works (and what doesn't) once and for all. Why? Because after an awesome, inspiring stint with Harley Davidson and Tony Robbins, Amy figured out what she really loves: helping small business owners like you break down BIG, powerful strategies into step-by-step actions...so you can see BIG, powerful results, fast.

Listen Money Matters
Host: Andrew Fiebert and Thomas Frank
Frequency: Weekly
Average Show Length: 50 Minutes

Description:
Honest and uncensored - this is not your father's boring finance show. This show brings much needed ACTIONABLE advice to a generation that hates being lectured about personal finance from the out-of-touch one percent. Andrew and Thomas are relatable, funny, and brash. Their down-to-earth discussions about money are entertaining whether you're a financial whiz or just starting out.

Manager Tools
Host: Mike Auzenne and Mark Horstman
Frequency: Weekly
Average Show Length: 30 Minutes

Description:
Tired of management theory? Want to learn specific skills to help improve your management performance? Then Manager Tools is the podcast for you! Manager Tools is a weekly business podcast focused on helping professionals become more effective managers and leaders. Each week, we discuss specific actions for professionals to take to achieve their desired management and career objectives. Manager Tools won Best Business Podcast Award in 2006, 2007, 2008, and 2012 as well as the People's Choice Award in 2008.

Motley Fool Money
Host: Various
Frequency: Weekly
Average Show Length: 40 Minutes

Description:
The "Motley Fool Money" radio show airs each week on stations across America, including top-10 markets Los Angeles, San Francisco, Atlanta, Boston and Washington, DC. The show features a team of Motley Fool analysts discussing the week's top business and investing stories, interviews, and an inside look at the stocks on our radar.

The Clark Howard Podcast

Host: Clark Howard
Frequency: Weekly
Average Show Length: 60 Minutes

Description:
Nationally-syndicated consumer expert Clark Howard shows you practical money-saving ideas to help you Save More, Spend Less, and Avoid Ripoffs.

This Is Your Life

Host: Michael Hyatt
Frequency: Weekly
Average Show Length: 30 Minutes

Description:
This Is Your Life with Michael Hyatt is a weekly podcast dedicated to intentional leadership. The goal is to help you live with more passion, work with greater focus, and lead with extraordinary influence.

The James Altucher Show

Host: James Altucher
Frequency: Weekly
Average Show Length: 90 Minutes

Description:
James Altucher is a successful entrepreneur, investor, board member, and the writer of 11 books including the recent WSJ Bestseller, "Choose Yourself!" (foreword by Dick Costolo, CEO of Twitter). He has started and sold several companies for eight figure exits. He's on the board of a billion revenue company, has written for The Financial Times, The New York Observer, and over a dozen popular websites for the past 15 years. He's run several hedge funds, venture capital funds, and is a successful angel investor in technology, energy, and biotech. He has also lost all his money, made it back, lost it, made it back several times and openly discusses how he did it in his columns and books.

Social Media Marketing Podcast
Host: Michael Stelzner
Frequency: Weekly
Average Show Length: 45 Minutes

Description:
Social Media Examiner's Michael Stelzner helps your business navigate the social jungle with success stories and expert interviews from leading social media marketing pros. Discover how successful businesses employ social media, learn new strategies and tactics, and gain actionable tips to improve your social media marketing.

Being Boss
Host: Emily Thompson and Kathleen Shannon
Frequency: Weekly
Average Show Length: 60 Minutes

Description:
Being boss is owning who you are and making things happen. Emily Thompson and Kathleen Shannon believe in building a business you love, making bank, and being unapologetically who you are 100% of the time. They have a combined experience and expertise in branding and coaching small online businesses to be more boss in work and life by focusing on "boss" mindsets, habits & routines, tools, tactics & strategies, blended with a little bit of hustle.

Getting Things Done
Host: Dave Allen
Frequency: Weekly
Average Show Length: 45 Minutes

Description:
Our GTD podcasts are here to support you at every stage of your GTD practice. You will hear interviews with people from all walks of life about their journey with GTD, from beginners to those who have been at it for years. The podcasts include personal and professional stories, as well as practical tips about GTD systems for desktop and mobile, using apps and paper. Start listening now and you'll be well on your way to stress-free productivity.

Mad Money
Host: Jim Cramer
Frequency: Weekly
Average Show Length: 45 Minutes

Description:
"Mad Money w/ Jim Cramer", which airs weeknights at 6pm on CNBC, takes viewers inside the mind of one of Wall Street's most respected and successful money managers. Jim is your personal guide through the confusing jungle of Wall Street investing, navigating th rough opportunities and pitfalls with one goal in mind - to help you make money. These full-length episodes feature the unmatched, fiery opinions of Jim Cramer and the popular "Lightning Round," in which Cramer gives his buy, sell, and hold opinions on stocks to callers.

Optimal Finance Daily
Host: Various
Frequency: Daily
Average Show Length: 45 Minutes

Description:
Why bother searching for the best blogs about personal finance when it can be found and read for you? Think of Optimal Finance Daily as an audioblog or blogcast. Optimal Finance Daily is a podcast created for those looking to improve their financial lives one step at a time: lifelong learners and life optimizers. We bring you the best content from blogs and other resources and read it to you, so that you don't have to waste your time finding and reading blogs yourself--listen during your commute, workout, regular routines, or during your down time 7 days a week and improve your life one step at a time. Each episode brings you a reading from a popular blog post or resource--practical and actionable information that has been proven to be worthy of large audiences.

Paychecks & Balances
Hosts: Rich & Marcus
Frequency: Weekly
Average Show Length: 60 Minutes

Description:
Rich & Marcus help you get it together financially and professionally without boring you to sleep. This podcast is for the rising professional interested in a light-hearted approach to personal finance and career development. Tune in every Tuesday for the latest episode.

Money Girl Quick and Dirty Tips
Host: Laura Adams
Frequency: Weekly
Average Show Length: 20 Minutes

Description:
Money Girl provides short and friendly personal finance, real estate, and investing tips to help you live a richer life. Whether you're just starting out or are already a savvy investor, Money Girl's advice will point you in the right direction.

Radical Personal Finance
Host: Joshua J Sheats
Frequency: Daily
Average Show Length: 60 Minutes

Description:
Joshua J Sheats, MSFS, CFP, CLU, ChFC, CASL, CAP, RHU, REBC is a financial planner who teaches people how to live a rich life now while building a plan for financial freedom in 10 years or less. He mixes creative approaches to lifestyle design, deep-dive financial planning techniques, and hard-core business strategy to equip you with the knowledge and inspiration you need to build financial independence.

Building A Story Brand
Host: Donald Miller
Frequency: Daily
Average Show Length: 50 Minutes

Description:
If you're frustrated because you struggle to get the word out about your product or service, the Building a Story Brand Podcast will help. Fans of the podcast are ecstatic about the fun and entertaining way Donald Miller brings you practical advice about clarifying your message and growing your business. Don and the StoryBrand team are the world's leading experts in harnessing the 2,000 year-old proven power of story formulas to get people talking about your brand. Get your message out, grow your company, stand out in the marketplace, and have a blast doing it!

COMEDY

2017 Comedy Top Pick
MY FAVORITE MURDER
Hosts: Karen Kilgariff and Georgia Hardstark
Frequency: Weekly
Average Show Length: 90 Minutes

Ready yourself for a murder adventure hosted by Karen Kilgariff and Georgia Hardstark, two lifelong fans of true crime stories. Each episode the girls tell each other their favorite tales of murder, and hear hometown crime stories from friends and fans. Check your anxiety at the door, cause Karen & Georgia are dying to discuss death.

Wait Wait... Don't Tell Me!
Host: Peter Sagal
Frequency: Weekly
Average Show Length: 50 Minutes

Description:
NPR's weekly current events quiz. Have a laugh and test your news knowledge while figuring out what's real and what we've made up.

The Joe Rogan Experience
Host: Joe Rogan
Frequency: Daily
Average Show Length: 180 Minutes

Description:
The podcast of comedian and UFC commentator Joe Rogan.

2 Dope Queens

Hosts: Phoebe Robinson and Jessica Williams
Frequency: Weekly
Average Show Length: 50 Minutes

Description:
Phoebe Robinson and Jessica Williams are funny. They're black. They're BFFs. And they host a live comedy show in Brooklyn. Join the 2 Dope Queens, along with their favorite comedians, for stories about sex, romance, race, hair journeys, living in New York, and Billy Joel. Plus a whole bunch of other s**t. WNYC Studios is the producer of other leading podcasts including Radiolab, Death, Sex & Money, Freakonomics Radio, Note to Self and many more.

Truth & Iliza

Hosts: Iliza Shlesinger
Frequency: Weekly
Average Show Length: 70 Minutes

Description
Henry Rollins once said "Nothing brings people together more than mutual hatred"- and Iliza Shlesinger believes that. It's the driving force behind war, political movements, and trickling all the way down to a really good cat fight on an episode of Real Housewives. Iliza believes that there is too much positivity in the world and we all get excited for things that make us happy for moments, but ultimately fade. "Truth and Iliza" believes that anger lasts longer than love; and sometimes anger can create a beautiful thing. Join Iliza Shlesinger and her friends talk about all the things that bother them on "Truth and Iliza" every week!

The Nerdist

Hosts: Chris Hardwick
Frequency: Weekly
Average Show Length: 120 Minutes

Description:
I am Chris Hardwick. I am on TV a lot and have a blog at nerdist.com. This podcast is basically just me talking about stuff and things with my two nerdy friends Jonah Ray and Matt Mira, and usually someone more famous than all of us. Occasionally we swear because that is fun. I hope you like it, but if you don't I'm sure you will not hesitate to unfurl your rage in the 'reviews' section because that's how the Internet works.

Welcome to Night Vale
Narrator: Cecil Baldwin
Frequency: Bi-Weekly
Average Show Length: 30 Minutes

Description:
Twice-monthly community updates for the small desert town of Night Vale, featuring local weather, news, announcements from the Sheriff's Secret Police, mysterious lights in the night sky, dark hooded figures with unknowable powers, and cultural events. Turn on your radio and hide. Never listened before? It's an ongoing radio show. Start with the current episode, and you'll catch on in no time. Or, go right to Episode 1 if you wanna binge-listen. (Produced by Night Vale Presents. Written by Joseph Fink and Jeffrey Cranor. Narrated by Cecil Baldwin. On Twitter as NightValeRadio)

Last Podcast On The Left
Hosts: Ben Kissel, Marcus Parks, Henry Zebrowski
Frequency: Weekly
Average Show Length: 70 Minutes

Description:
The Last Podcast On The Left covers all the horrors our world has to offer both imagined and real, from demons and slashers to cults and serial killers, The Last Podcast is guaranteed to satisfy your bloodlust. Also, a complete archive of TLPOTL can be found at cavecomedyradio.com!

Always Open
Host: Barbara Dunkelman
Frequency: Weekly
Average Show Length: 50 Minutes

Description:
Join Barbara Dunkelman and friends every week as they sit down for a late night chat at their favorite diner to talk about life, love, sex, and everything in between.

Guys We F****d
Host: Corinne Fisher, Krystyna Hutchinson
Frequency: Weekly
Average Show Length: 120 Minutes

Description:
Welcome to GUYS WE F****D: THE ANTI SLUT-SHAMING PODCAST. They spread their legs, now they're spreading the word that women should be able to have sex with WHOEVER they want WHENEVER they want and not be ashamed or called sluts or whores. Welcome to a new revolution. Each week, Corinne Fisher & Krystyna Hutchinson (together known as the comedy duo Sorry About Last Night) interview a gentleman they slept with. Some they made love to, some they had sex with a few times and some they f****d in a hotel bathroom...er, what? Corinne & Krystyna want to make the world a more sex-positive place...one candid story of intercourse at a time.

Bill Burr's Monday Morning Podcast
Host: Bill Burr
Frequency: Weekly
Average Show Length: 120 Minutes

Description:
Bill Burr rants about relationship advice, sports and the Illuminati.

Tax Season
Host: Taxtone
Frequency: Weekly
Average Show Length: 90 Minutes

Description:
The only show bringing you an unfiltered view from the streets of Brooklyn as only Taxstone knows them.

Shane and Friends
Host: Shane Dawson
Frequency: Weekly
Average Show Length: 60 Minutes

Description:
I'm Shane Dawson and I have a lot of friends. Most of them are in my head. Listen as me and my producer Lauren Schnipper talk about stuff we think is funny and interview people we hope are funny. Also I like to

do character voices and celebrity impressions but I promise, it's not as annoying as it sounds.

Sucks Radio
Hosts: Mark Dawson, Stone Manson
Frequency: Daily
Average Show Length: 30 Minutes

Description:
Mr.D has always wanted to alter other people's sucky lives by dangling a carrot to see change, and this popular podcast format has that potential. After writing the book, When It Sucks It Blows, he felt he needed to fill in the blanks, as in, from his empty noodle, and this funny podcast can help define and further add to the crap that has laid waste to his back forty, IQ, that is! It's only 30 minutes of craziness that leads to rehab, a local bar or some lumpy couch to find solace. That's not much straining to maintain for a freebee, don't ya think? And working for the man has to be the cause and affect to validate time listening to Sucks Radio. Let his soothing, hypnotic and charming wit take you on a journey to some courthouse to file a lawsuit against Amway or Mary Kay. With Stone Manson and V 1.3 in the Silo everyday to juggle, swallow fire and tame all those mangy tigers, it's one chaotic experience after another and it maybe one of the best iTunes podcast to ever grace Mamma Earth, you be the judge and jury!

The Dollop
Host: Dave Anthony, Gareth Reynolds
Frequency: Weekly
Average Show Length: 60 Minutes

Description:
Comedians Dave Anthony and Gareth Reynolds pick a subject from history and examine it.

Comedy Central Stand-Up
Host: Various
Frequency: Weekly
Average Show Length: 15 Minutes

Description:
CC:Stand-Up is the digital home for stand-up comedy, comedians and your mom.

Ask Me Another
Host: Ophira Eisenberg
Frequency: Weekly
Average Show Length: 50 Minutes

Description:
Ask Me Another brings the lively spirit and healthy competition of your favorite trivia night right to your ears. With a rotating cast of funny people, puzzle writers and VIP guests, it features the wit of host Ophira Eisenberg, the music of house musician Jonathan Coulton, and rambunctious trivia games, all played in front of a live audience.

Chive Podcast
Host: John Resig, Bob Phillipp
Frequency: Weekly
Average Show Length: 60 Minutes

Description:
theCHIVE...now with words! John Resig and Bob Phillipp deliver a weekly dose of the Chive Culture. Expect off-the-wall interviews with celebrity guests, quirky news headlines, and questions you may or may not want answered. Everything's up for grabs, so who knows what's going to happen. The Chive Podcast: Probably the best podcast in the world.

I Tell My Husband The News
Hosts: Shannon Green, Dusty Terrill
Frequency: Weekly
Average Show Length: 15 Minutes

Description:
Shannon Green, a journalist at USA TODAY, tells her husband Dusty Terrill, a local comedian, the news stories of the week that he most likely missed in this weekly podcast.

How Did This Get Made
Hosts: Paul Scheer, June Diane Raphael, Jason Mantzoukas
Frequency: Weekly
Average Show Length: 180 Minutes

Description:
Have you ever seen a movie so bad that it's amazing? Paul Scheer, June Diane Raphael and Jason Mantzoukas want to hear about it! We'll watch it with our funniest friends, and report back to you with the results.

Anna Faris Is Unqualified
Host: Anna Faris
Frequency: Weekly
Average Show Length: 60 Minutes

Description:
Not-great-relationship advice from completely unqualified Hollywood types. I am a solid 3.4 student with a major in English from the University of Washington. I've also been asked what my SAT score was and it was 1060. It only took five years of dorm/rave life for me to accrue the life knowledge I have received. I'm a Sagittarius, which means I'm super creative and stubborn; but there are walls I need to break down because I always want to leap over the boundaries that make me climb ladders and roofs. I'm agreeable and delightful. I also have incredible leadership skills and following abilities. And, I have 20/20 vision so I'm an eagle eye.

Norm Macdonald Live
Host: Norm Macdonald
Frequency: Weekly
Average Show Length: 180 Minutes

Description:
Norm Macdonald comes to the internet in his all-new weekly podcast, Norm Macdonald Live. Every Monday, trusty sidekick Adam Eget joins Norm as they discuss the day's top stories, talk with their famous guests and friends, and answer live fan-submitted questions.

Betch Slapped
Hosts: The Betches
Frequency: Weekly
Average Show Length: 30 Minutes

Description:
Stand Up NY Labs presents Betch Slapped- a hilarious weekly podcast hosted by the founders of Betches and comedic authors behind NY Times best-selling books "Nice is Just a Place in France" and "I Had a Nice Time & Other Lies." You'll hear the Betches' take on everything from celebrity gossip to what you should be watching on TV to actual news that you might give a sh*t about. You'll also get to hear The Betches give advice to listeners about love, friendship, and other sh*t in "Dear Betch" and join them as they play riveting games like "Shoot, F*ck, Marry."

My Brother, My Brother and Me
Hosts: Justin McElroy, Travis McElroy, Griffin McElroy
Frequency: Weekly
Average Show Length: 60 Minutes

Description:
Free advice from three of the world's most qualified, most related experts:
Justin, Travis and Griffin McElroy. For one-half to three-quarters of an
hour every Monday, we tell people how to live their lives, because we're
obviously doing such a great job of it so far.

Comedy Bang Bang: The Podcast
Hosts: Scott Aukerman
Frequency: Weekly
Average Show Length: 60 Minutes

Description:
Join host Scott Aukerman ("Comedy Bang! Bang!" on IFC, "Mr. Show") for a
weekly podcast that blends conversation and character work from today's
funniest comedians. While Scott begins by traditionally interviewing
the celebrities, the open-door policy means an assortment of eccentric
oddballs can pop by at any moment to chat, compete in games, and
engage in comic revelry. With all that,and regular bonus episodes, we bet
your favorite part will still be the plugs!

We Got This with Mark and Hal
Hosts: Mark Gagliardi, Hal Lublin
Frequency: Weekly
Average Show Length: 60 Minutes

Description:
Each week, actors Mark Gagliardi and Hal Lublin (Drunk History, The
Thrilling Adventure Hour, Welcome to Night Vale) sit down to settle all the
small debates that are a big deal to YOU - once and for all. No subject is
too small for Mark and Hal to tackle! Even though you may think it's an
impossible puzzle to solve, don't worry... We Got This.

Not Too Deep with Grace Helbig
Host: Grace Helbig
Frequency: Weekly
Average Show Length: 60 Minutes

Description:
You know those podcasts where famous people recount their lives and careers, and then things get emotional? That is NOT this show! Hosted by internet superstar Grace Helbig, "Not Too Deep" is a ridiculous, silly, and unapologetically superficial interview podcast, that is more about the laffs than about the feels.

You Made It Weird with Pete
Host: Pete Holmes
Frequency: Weekly
Average Show Length: 180 Minutes

Description:
Everybody has secret weirdness, Pete Holmes gets comedians to share theirs.

APM: A Prairie Home Companion News from Lake Wobergon
Host: Garrison Keillor
Frequency: Weekly
Average Show Length: 15 Minutes

Description:
Garrison Keillor's signature monologue, The News from Lake Wobegon, a staple of the live public radio program A Prairie Home Companion.

The Adventure Zone
Hosts: Justin McElroy, Travis McElroy, Griffin McElroy
Frequency: Weekly
Average Show Length: 60 Minutes

Description:
Justin, Travis and Griffin McElroy from My Brother, My Brother and Me have recruited their dad Clint for a campaign of high adventure. Join the McElroys as they find their fortune and slay an unconscionable number of ... you know, kobolds or whatever in ... The Adventure Zone.

Beautiful Stories From Anonymous People
Hosts: Chris Gethard
Frequency: Weekly
Average Show Length: 60 Minutes

Description:
1 phone call. 1 hour. No names. No holds barred. Thats the premise behind Beautiful Stories from Anonymous People, hosted by comedian Chris Gethard (the Chris Gethard Show, Broad City, This American Life, and one of Time Outs "10 best comedians of 2015"). Every week, Chris opens the phone line to one anonymous caller, and he can't hang up first, no matter what. From shocking confessions and family secrets to philosophical discussions and shameless self-promotion, anything can and will happen!

Here We Are
Hosts: Shane Mauss
Frequency: Weekly
Average Show Length: 60 Minutes

Description:
Join comedian Shane Mauss as he interviews science experts across the country in a journey to find out what makes us who we are.

The Basement Yard
Hosts: Shane Mauss
Frequency: Weekly
Average Show Length: 45 Minutes

Description:
The Basement Yard is a podcast ran by me, Joe Santagato. I would write a long description about what this podcast will be about but I'm not even sure.. Enjoy!

The Sex, Drugs & Rock N' Roll Show
Hosts: Big Jay Oakerson, Ralph Sutton
Frequency: Twice Weekly
Average Show Length: 90 Minutes

Description:
The SDR Show (Sex, Drugs, & Rock-n-Roll) is a one hour weekly podcast featuring comedian Big Jay Oakerson and radio host Ralph Sutton. Each week they interview Porn Stars, Rock Stars, and more. Big Jay Oakerson has been on the stand up circuit for over a decade. Has had his own

comedy special on comedy central, was the opening act for Korn on the Rockstar Energy Tour as well as many various TV shows and comedy tours. Ralph Sutton has been the host of a nationally syndicated rock radio show for over a decade, has been a VJ on VH1-Classic as well as the host on various tv shows as well as of Shiprocked, M3 Rock Festival, and the Sturgis Motorcycle rally.

Bitch Sesh: A Real Housewives Breakdown
Hosts: Casey Wilson and Danielle Schneider
Frequency: Weekly
Average Show Length: 45 Minutes

Description:
Casey Wilson and Danielle Schneider (Hotwives Of Las Vegas) LOVE the Real Housewives on Bravo, and they're sharing that excitement with you on Bitch Sesh! Listen in to hear the ladies dish on the seasons wildest moments, answer to all your burning Housewives questions, drink Housewives-branded wine, and bring on some super special guests. Don't be tardy to the party!

Alison Rosen Is Your New Best Friend
Hosts: Alison Rosen
Frequency: Weekly
Average Show Length: 45 Minutes

Description:
A twice weekly podcast hosted by veteran interviewer and everyone's new best friend, Alison Rosen, featuring surprisingly honest conversations that are equal parts silly, serious, revelatory and sometimes involving a sombrero. Plus an eternal quest to find out if that thing you think or do is normal in a segment called "Just Me or Everyone?"

Rooster Teeth Podcast
Hosts: Gus Sorola, Burnie Burns, Barbara Dunkelman, Gavin Free
Frequency: Weekly
Average Show Length: 180 Minutes

Description:
On a more or less weekly basis the Rooster Teeth crew discuss gaming, films, and projects that they're currently working on.

Sawbones: A Marital Tour of Misguided Medicine
Hosts: Dr. Sydnee McElroy, Justin McElroy
Frequency: Weekly
Average Show Length: 45 Minutes

Description:
Join Dr. Sydnee McElroy and her husband Justin McElroy for a tour of all the dumb, bad, gross, weird and wrong ways we've tried to fix people.

Hello From The Magic Tavern
Hosts: Arnie Niekamp
Frequency: Weekly
Average Show Length: 45 Minutes

Description:
Hi. I'm Arnie. I fell through a portal behind a Burger King into the magical land of Foon. I'm still trying to get my bearings, but I have my podcasting gear and get a weak WiFi signal from the Burger King so I figured I might as well set up shop at the nearby inn and interview some people. When in Foon...

The Adam and Dr. Drew Show
Hosts: Adam Carolla, Dr. Drew Pinsky
Frequency: Weekly
Average Show Length: 30 Minutes

Description:
Adam Carolla & Dr. Drew Pinsky reunite the partnership that made Loveline a wild success and cultural touchstone. In each episode Adam and Drew take uncensored, nothing-off-limits, calls about sex, drug, medical and relationship issues. Dr. Drew brings the medicine while Adam's comedy and rants are the spoonful of sugar to make it go down.

The Duncan Trussel Family Hour
Hosts: Duncan Trussel
Frequency: Weekly
Average Show Length: 90 Minutes

Description:
A weekly salon-style supershow, where comedian Duncan Trussell and guests explore the outer reaches of the multiverse.

Psychobabble
Hosts: Tyler Oakley, Korey Kuhl
Frequency: Weekly
Average Show Length: 45 Minutes

Description:
It's not just crazy talk, it's Psychobabble - the official free audio podcast from YouTube sensation Tyler Oakley. Listen each week as he and his bestie Korey Kuhl bring you a half hour of unfiltered gossip sessions, pop culture scrutiny, and stories never told before.

KFC Radio
Hosts: Tyler Oakley, Korey Kuhl
Frequency: Weekly
Average Show Length: 45 Minutes

Description:
Featuring all of the regular Barstool personalities, KFC Radio is the quintessential bar conversation brought to podcast form. Listener interaction is the name of the game as Barstool readers and listeners contribute their Stoolie Voicemails to drive the conversation to strange places including embarrassing personal stories, bizarre hypothetical questions, and more. New episodes of the hilarious Barstool Network flagship show are released every Friday.

The Church of What's Happening Now
Host: Joey Coco Diaz
Frequency: Twice Weekly
Average Show Length: 180 Minutes

Description:
The Church Of What's Happening Now With: Joey Coco Diaz is a twice-weekly podcast hosted by Comedian Joey Coco Diaz along with his co-host Lee Syatt. Joey doesn't hold anything back and let's you know exactly what's on his mind. Joey and Lee are joined by one of Joey's friends, Comedians, Actors, Writers and Director's to name a few. We look forward to having you as a member of The Church.

Doug Loves Movies

Host: Doug Benson
Frequency: Weekly
Average Show Length: 90 Minutes

Description:
Comedian Doug Benson (Super High Me, Last Comic Standing) invites his friends to sit down and discuss his first love: movies!

EDUCATION

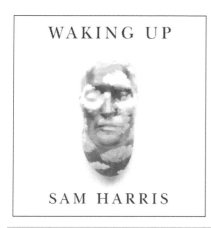

WAKING UP

SAM HARRIS

2017 Education Top Pick
WAKING UP
Hosts: Sam Harris
Frequency: Weekly
Average Show Length:
90 Minutes

Join neuroscientist, philosopher, and best-selling author Sam Harris as he explores important and controversial questions about the human mind, society, and current events. Sam Harris is the author of The End of Faith, Letter to a Christian Nation, The Moral Landscape, and more.

TEDTalks Audio
Host: Various
Frequency: Daily
Average Show Length: 15 Minutes

Description:
TED is a nonprofit devoted to Ideas Worth Spreading. On this feed, you'll find TEDTalks video to inspire, intrigue and stir the imagination from some of the world's leading thinkers and doers, speaking from the stage at TED conferences, TEDx events and partner events around the world. This podcast is also available in high-def video and audio-only formats.

The Tony Robbins Podcast
Host: Tony Robbins
Frequency: Weekly
Average Show Length: 50 Minutes

Description:
Tony Robbins, the #1 Life and Business Strategist, has helped over 50 million people from 100 countries create real and lasting change in their lives. In this podcast, he shares proven strategies and tactics so you, too, can achieve massive results in your business, relationships, health and finances.

Grammar Girl Quick and Dirty Tips
Host: Mignon Fogarty
Frequency: Weekly
Average Show Length: 15 Minutes

Description:
Grammar Girl provides short, friendly tips to improve your writing. Whether English is your first language or your second language, these grammar, punctuation, style, and business tips will make you a better and more successful writer. Grammar Girl is a Quick and Dirty Tips podcast.

Coffee Break Spanish
Host: Mark Pentleton
Frequency: Weekly
Average Show Length: 15 Minutes

Description:
Learn Spanish with Coffee Break Spanish, bringing you language-learning with your latte! Aimed at total beginners, this podcast will help you get to grips with the Spanish language.

Surprisingly Awesome
Host: Rachel Ward
Frequency: Monthly
Average Show Length: 40 Minutes

Description:
Taking on subjects that appear boring and explaining why they're actually awesome.

American Conservative University Podcast
Host: Various
Frequency: Daily
Average Show Length: 90 Minutes

Description:
All free!! All educational. All entertaining. All professionally recorded. No empty rhetoric here. Just entertaining learning. Choose from many different topics from the best talent around the world. Earn your American Conservative Masters Degree just by listening. No writing, no assignments. Just listen at the feet of some of the world's greatest Conservative thinkers.

CodeNewbie

Host: Various
Frequency: Daily
Average Show Length: 60 Minutes

Description:
Stories and interviews from people on their coding journey.

TED-Ed: Lessons Worth Sharing

Host: Various
Frequency: Daily
Average Show Length: 5 Minutes

Description:
TED-Ed's commitment to creating lessons worth sharing is an extension of TED's mission of spreading great ideas. Within TED-Ed's growing library of TED-Ed animations, you will find carefully curated educational videos, many of which represent collaborations between talented educators and animators nominated through the TED-Ed website (ed.ted.com).

French Podcast

Host: Various
Frequency: Weekly
Average Show Length: 10 Minutes

Description:
Learn French online with us! In our course we emphasize all aspects of language learning from listening comprehension, rapid vocabulary expansion, exposure to French grammar and common idiomatic expressions, to pronunciation practice and interactive grammar exercises. In our program we discuss the Weekly News, French grammar, and French expressions, and much more in simplified French at a slow pace so that you can understand almost every word and sentence.

Learn French with Daily Podcasts
Host: Various
Frequency: Daily
Average Show Length: 5 Minutes

Description:
Learn French with free daily podcasts, brought to you by French teachers from Paris. DailyFrenchPod is an amazing effective and new way to learn French, combining daily podcast, a daily learning guide including review exercises, PDF transcript, keywords, audio and PDF vocabulary sheets, grammar tutorials, and a large community of students and experts to practice with.

EconTalk
Host: Russ Roberts
Frequency: Weekly
Average Show Length: 60 Minutes

Description:
EconTalk is an award-winning weekly talk show about economics in daily life. Featured guests include renowned economics professors, Nobel Prize winners, and exciting speakers on all kinds of topical matters related to economic thought. Topics include health care, business cycles, economic growth, free trade, education, finance, politics, sports, book reviews, parenting, and the curiosities of everyday decision-making. Russ Roberts, of the Library of Economics and Liberty (econlib.org) and the Hoover Institution, draws you in with lively guests and creative repartee.

Entrepreneurial Thought Leaders
Host: Various
Frequency: Weekly
Average Show Length: 60 Minutes

Description:
The DFJ Entrepreneurial Thought Leaders Seminar (ETL) is a weekly seminar series on entrepreneurship, co-sponsored by BASES (a student entrepreneurship group), Stanford Technology Ventures Program, and the Department of Management Science and Engineering.

TEDTalks Education
Host: Various
Frequency: Monthly
Average Show Length: 20 Minutes

Description:
What should future schools look like? How do brains learn? Some of the world's greatest educators, researchers, and community leaders share their stories and visions onstage at the TED conference, TEDx events and partner events around the world.

The Majority Report with Sam Seder
Host: Sam Seder
Frequency: Daily
Average Show Length: 90 Minutes

Description:
The Majority Report is not for everyone. However, if you genuinely want to understand policy and how politics impact our lives, this is your show. This daily podcast features long form interviews of authors, economists, journalists, activists and politicians. If you're a fan of Dan Carlin or New Yorker's Politics show or even Rachel Maddow, the Majority Report is a daily must listen. Hosted by Sam Seder, the Majority Report is a thoughtful and entertaining analysis of the policies, politics and social dynamics that shape our lives.

Explain Things To Me
Hosts: Anna Akana and Brad Gage
Frequency: Weekly
Average Show Length: 40 Minutes

Description:
Hosts Anna Akana and Brad Gage sit down with experts to discuss their various fields.

English as a Second Language

Host: Various
Frequency: Weekly
Average Show Length: 30 Minutes

Description:
English as a Second Language Podcast is for anyone who wants to improve their English speaking and listening skills.

Psychology in Everyday Life: The Psych Files

Host: Michael Britt
Frequency: Weekly
Average Show Length: 20 Minutes

Description:
The Psych Files is a podcast for anyone interested in the topic of psychology and how ideas in this field apply to everyday life. Michael Britt brings you an upbeat, fun podcast of interest to everyone from psychology majors to those just interested in why people do what they do.

Learn German - GermanPod101.com

Host: Various
Frequency: Weekly
Average Show Length: 5 Minutes

Description:
GermanPod101.com is an innovative and fun way of learning the German language and culture at your own convenience and pace. Our language training system consists of free daily podcast audio lessons, video lessons, German Word of the Day, a premium learning center, and a vibrant user community.

History of Philosophy Without Any Gaps

Host: Peter Adamson
Frequency: Weekly
Average Show Length: 30 Minutes

Description:
Peter Adamson, Professor of Philosophy at the LMU in Munich and at King's College London, takes listeners through the history of philosophy, "without any gaps." The series looks at the ideas, lives and historical context of the major philosophers as well as the lesser-known figures of the tradition.

Slate Presents Lexicon Valley
Host: Bob Garfield
Frequency: Weekly
Average Show Length: 30 Minutes

Description:
Lexicon Valley is a podcast about language, from pet peeves, syntax, and etymology to neurolinguistics and the death of languages. Your hosts are Bob Garfield and producer Mike Vuolo. Part of the Panoply Network.

Hello Internet
Host: CGP Grey and Brady Haran
Frequency: Weekly
Average Show Length: 90 Minutes

Description:
CGP Grey and Brady Haran talk about YouTube, life, work, whatever.

You Need A Budget
Host: Jesse Mecham
Frequency: Weekly
Average Show Length: 5 Minutes

Description:
A weekly dose of just the right medicine to help you get out of debt, save more money, and beat the paycheck to paycheck cycle.

JavaScript Jabber
Host: Charles Wood
Frequency: Weekly
Average Show Length: 60 Minutes

Description:
Weekly podcast discussion about Javascript on the front and back ends. Also discuss programming practices, coding environments, and the communities related to the technology.

School Sucks
Host: Brett Veinotte
Frequency: Weekly
Average Show Length: 90 Minutes

Description:
Know yourself. Teach yourself. Improve yourself. School Sucks is a
podcast, call-in show, You Tube channel, & web community promoting real
education and rooting out indoctrination. We discuss home-education, self-
education, critical thinking, self knowledge, peaceful parenting, personal
growth, nonviolent communication & non-aggression.

Hillsdale Dialogues Podcast
Host: Larry P. Arnn
Frequency: Weekly
Average Show Length: 35 Minutes

Description:
A survey of great books, great men, and great ideas. Larry P. Arnn,
president of Hillsdale College, on the Hugh Hewitt Show

London School of Economics: Public Lectures and Events
Host: Various
Frequency: Weekly
Average Show Length: 60 Minutes

Description:
Audio podcasts from LSE's programme of public lectures and events.

Smart People Podcast
Host: Chris Semp
Frequency: Weekly
Average Show Length: 60 Minutes

Description:
Smart People Podcast is simply a place to hear cool stuff from some of the
smartest people on earth. We are reaching out to leading professionals in
various industries to pick their oversized brains and pass that information
along to our listeners. You will hear top notch advice from M.D.'s and CFP's,
athletes and intellectuals, porn stars and Buddhists and everything in
between.

The Torch: The Great Courses Podcast
Host: Various
Frequency: Monthly
Average Show Length: 30 Minutes

Description:
The Great Courses brings engaging professors from the best universities to our learners, creating a "university of the best" with our customers participating in every step of the process. With this podcast hosted by Ed Leon, you'll meet our fascinating professors and experts who create The Great Courses, listen to their stories and insights, and learn more about the great work they are doing. Discover scientists explaining the latest findings from the fields of astronomy, particle physics, or neuroscience; historians exploring the implications of the latest archaeological findings; medical experts making sense of current health alerts or medical breakthroughs; and literature professors bringing fresh insights to classic literary works.

GAMES & HOBBIES

CAR TALK

Hosts: Tom Magliozzi
and Ray Magliozzi
Frequency: Weekly
Average Show Length:
50 Minutes

America's funniest auto mechanics take calls from weary car owners all over the country, and crack wise while they diagnose Dodges and dismiss Diahatsus. You don't have to know anything about cars to love this one hour weekly laugh fest.

CoolGames Inc
Hosts: Griffin McElroy and Nick Robinson
Frequency: Weekly
Average Show Length: 60 Minutes

Description
Join Griffin McElroy and Nick Robinson as they create a new video game every week – with your help.

Waypoint Radio
Hosts: Austin Walker and Patrick Klepek
Frequency: Daily
Average Show Length: 60 Minutes

Description
What's good, Internet? Join VICE Gaming's Austin Walker and Patrick Klepek twice a week, as they break down the biggest stories in video games and unfairly compare everything to Dark Souls.

Giant Bombcast
Host: Brad Shoemaker
Frequency: Daily
Average Show Length: 60 Minutes

Description
The Giant Bomb staff discuss the latest video game news and new releases, taste-test questionable beverages, and get wildly off-topic in this weekly podcast.

Unranked
Hosts: Christian Humes, Alex Marinello and Dan Weine
Frequency: Weekly
Average Show Length: 40 Minutes

Description
Join hosts Christian Humes, Alex Marinello, & Dan Weine, as they discuss games and the culture surrounding them. This is the show dedicated to endless nights of online matches, and countless rounds of split-screen classics. Play along in a variety of podcast games. Listen as they attempt to thread a narrative between titles like Sonic the Hedgehog and The Sims in Game-Link. Try and guess the true game description after being given a title in Game or No Game. Attempt to pick the IGN review scores for classic and obscure titles. These are a few of the fun games you can expect, and many more from the Unranked podcast.

Watch Our for Fireballs!
Hosts: Gary Butterfield and Kole Ross
Frequency: Weekly
Average Show Length: 120 Minutes

Description
Watch Out for Fireballs! is a game club podcast, focused on retro and non-current games. Every two weeks, we play a game in its entirety, then discuss its merits and flaws at length. Most episodes begin with a short sketch, and we're pretty liberal about keeping tangents in. But it ultimately comes down to: Why do we like (or dislike?) this game.

PS I Love You XOXO
Hosts: Greg Miller and Colin Moriarty
Frequency: Weekly
Average Show Length: 90 Minutes

Description
This is the podcast love letter to all things PlayStation that Greg Miller and Colin Moriarty were born to do. PS I Love You XOXO, every Tuesday 9AM PT.

Game Scoop!
Hosts: Daemon Hatfield and Justin Davis
Average Show Length: 90 Minutes

Description
IGN.com shoots a week's worth of gaming news straight into your ear!

Good Job, Brain!
Hosts: Karen Chu, Colin Felton, Dana Nelson and Chris Kohler
Frequency: Weekly
Average Show Length: 60 Minutes

Description
Part pub quiz show, part offbeat news, and all awesome. All the time! We here are nuts about trivia. And we are darn sure there are people out there who share our unusual obsession. Do you relish beating your friends at Trivial Pursuit? Do you blab out the answers at the gym when Jeopardy! is on? Then this podcast, fellow trivia nut, is the ultimate mental nutrition for your very big brain. So eat up!

Kinda Funny Gamescast
Hosts: Tim Gettys, Greg Miller, and Colin Moriarty
Frequency: Weekly
Average Show Length: 60 Minutes

Description
Every week Tim Gettys, Greg Miller, and Colin Moriarty talk about everything going on in the video game world. Sometimes there are guests, sometimes there is a wiener dog, all the times Tim will say something ridiculous.

The Patch
Hosts: Gustavo Sorola Burnie Burns, Ryan Haywood, Ashley Jenkins and
Meg Turney
Frequency: Weekly
Average Show Length: 60 Minutes

Description
With a combined 7,000 years of experience playing video games, the
Rooster Teeth crew is here to drop some serious gaming knowledge.

Podcast Beyond
Hosts: Various
Frequency: Weekly
Average Show Length: 60 Minutes

Description
The IGN PlayStation Team sits down and talks all things Sony, sprinkling
a little madness and song along the way. Podcast Beyond is the premiere
source for Sony news, opinions and old-fashioned shenanigans.

The Giant Beastcast
Host: Brad Shoemaker
Frequency: Weekly
Average Show Length: 120 Minutes

Description
The Giant Bomb East team gathers to talk about the week in video games,
their lives, and basically anything that interests them. All from New York
City!

Dude Soup
Host: Various
Frequency: Weekly
Average Show Length: 60 Minutes

Description
Jump in the Dude Soup -- all the gaming, nerd culture, and meat-packing
industry commentary you can handle.

IGN Games Podcasts
Hosts: Jose Otero and Peer Schneider
Frequency: Weekly
Average Show Length: 60 Minutes

Description
All of IGN.com's video game podcasts jammed into one feed. It's like one of those little clown cars, but for your ears.

Drunks and Dragons
Hosts: Various
Frequency: Weekly
Average Show Length: 60 Minutes

Description
Join us on our weekly podcast as our new group of adventurers learn the ropes in the Dungeons and Dragons universe.

Nintendo Voice Chat
Hosts: Various
Frequency: Weekly
Average Show Length: 60 Minutes

Description
IGN editors discuss all things Nintendo. Now you're playing with power!

The Game Informer Show
Host: Ben Hanson
Frequency: Weekly
Average Show Length: 90 Minutes

Description
Game Informer's staff break down the week's biggest releases, reveal exclusive information on exciting games on the horizon, respond to listener emails, play game-focused trivia, and interview the most interesting developers in the industry. Check it out!

The Co-Optional Podcast

Host: TotalBiscuit, Dodger and Jesse Cox
Frequency: Weekly
Average Show Length: 180 Minutes

Description
Home of the Co-optional podcast, an irreverent gaming show hosted by TotalBiscuit, Dodger and Jesse Cox. Here you will also find TotalBiscuits irregular audio-blogs.

The Smoking Tire

Hosts: Matt Farah, Zack Klapman, Chris Hayes and Thad Brown
Frequency: Weekly
Average Show Length: 60 Minutes

Description
Matt Farah, Zack Klapman, Chris Hayes, and Thad Brown sit down with automotive icons, pro drivers, comedians and other friends to discuss automotive industry news, racing, projects and whatever else comes to mind.

The Instance

Hosts: Scott Johnson, Dills, and Turpster
Frequency: Weekly
Average Show Length: 90 Minutes

Description
The Instance: Weekly radio for fans and lovers of World of Warcraft. We don't take sides, we don't whine, we just give you the facts, news and tips that you want and need for your favorite online addiction. Come meet us at the stone for another Instance!

Car Stuff

Hosts: Ben Bowlin and Scott Benjamin
Frequency: Weekly
Average Show Length: 90 Minutes

Description
What's the history of stop lights? What are some common myths about car dealerships? Join Scott and Ben as they take a closer look at all things automotive in CarStuff, a podcast by HowStuffWorks.com.

Reclaimed Audio Podcast
Hosts: Phil Pinsky, Tim Sway and Bill Lutes
Frequency: Weekly
Average Show Length: 60 Minutes

Description
Weekly podcast that discusses upcycling and making with reclaimed materials.

The Indoor Kids
Hosts: Kumail Nanjiani and Emily V. Gordon
Frequency: Weekly
Average Show Length: 60 Minutes

Description
The Indoor Kids isn't just about video games, but it isn't not about video games. The Indoor Kids is all about the kind of lifestyle you have to lead in order to be a proper Gamer, capital G. Join hosts Kumail Nanjiani and Emily V. Gordon as they take on a journey from childhood Shinobi obsessions, up through the best and worst video game adaptations of movies. Grab your Energy Swords(Mountain Dew liter bottles)!

Dragon Talk
Hosts: Trevor Kidd, Shelly Mazzanoble and Greg Tito
Frequency: Weekly
Average Show Length: 60 Minutes

Description
Go inside the walls of Dungeons & Dragons for exclusive interviews and previews! The D&D team sits down each week with celebrities and personalities from across gaming and pop culture to discuss one of the greatest fantasy brands of all-time. We'll talk about the tabletop roleplaying game, as the latest in D&D video games, comics, novels, movies, and television, plus listen to our live play-throughs featuring Penny-Arcade's Acquisitions Incorporated.

Super Best Friendcast!
Hosts: Various
Frequency: Weekly
Average Show Length: 180 Minutes

Description
Every week, the creators of Two Best Friends Play discuss the best and worst of the videogame industry, pop culture and get excessively hyped about things for no reason.

Top Level Podcast
Hosts: Patrick Chapin with Michael J Flores
Frequency: Weekly
Average Show Length: 90 Minutes

Description
Top Level Podcast is a weekly podcast by Magic: The Gathering Pro Tour Hall of Famer and Pro Tour Champion Patrick Chapin with Michael J Flores. Top Level Podcast focuses on competitive, Constructed, tournament Magic: The Gathering strategy, tactics, deck lists, and mindset.

Retronauts
Hosts: Bob Mackey and Jeremy Parish
Frequency: Weekly
Average Show Length: 60 Minutes

Description
The world's favorite podcast about old video games reaches its next stage! Join Bob Mackey, Jeremy Parish, and a variety of guests as they discuss the favorite games and topics of yesteryear.

Critical Hit
Host: Various
Frequency: Weekly
Average Show Length: 90 Minutes

Description
Listen, learn, and laugh along with the members of the Critical Hit Podcast. The continuing saga of four adventurers seeking fortune and glory in the world of Dungeons and Dragons. Plenty of role playing and fun for anyone interested in the Dungeons and Dragons experience. Newbies or seasoned vets will get a kick out of this live campaign.

Car Cast

Hosts: Adam Carolla and Matt D'Andria
Frequency: Weekly
Average Show Length: 60 Minutes

Description
CarCast is an automotive podcast and Internet video series hosted by Adam Carolla and Matt D'Andria. It is the only show of its kind that explores all aspects of the automotive space with entertaining humor and expertise. The guys answer your questions, offer advice and feature the best new and custom-built rides. CarCast regularly features guests from the automotive industry and celebrity car enthusiasts.

It's Super Effective

Host: Steve Black Jr.
Frequency: Weekly
Average Show Length: 60 Minutes

Description
It's Super Effective is a Pokémon podcast that covers the Pokémon anime, the Pokémon movies, the video games (such as Pokémon Sun & Pokémon Moon), competitive Pokémon battling, the Pokémon TCG, Pokémon GO and more! It's Super Effective is an award-winning podcast, and the #1 most downloaded Pokémon podcast on the web. PKMNcast.com is dedicated to not only bringing exclusive, creative Pokémon content on the internet. To top that off, ISE is dedicated to bringing you weekly laughs and the best coverage of EVERYTHING Pokémon.

Wood Talk

Hosts: Marc Spagnuolo, Matt Vanderlist, and Shannon Rogers
Frequency: Weekly
Average Show Length: 30 Minutes

Description
A woodworking audio show geared toward the modern fine woodworker. Join your hosts Marc Spagnuolo, Matt Vanderlist, and Shannon Rogers for a light-hearted look at the latest news, tips, and tricks from the world of woodworking.

Crucible Radio
Host: Various
Frequency: Weekly
Average Show Length: 60 Minutes

Description
A show discussing all things Destiny Crucible - Strategies, tips, meta-game, map guides, loadouts, and more! Inspired by the subreddit r/CruciblePlaybook, Crucible Radio aims to be an additional resource for expanding your arsenal, improving your game, and getting more enjoyment out of Destiny's player vs. player content.

Kotaku Splitscreen
Hosts: Kirk Hamilton and Jason Schreier
Frequency: Weekly
Average Show Length: 60 Minutes

Description
Kotaku's Kirk Hamilton and Jason Schreier talk about all things gaming.

Podcast Unlocked
Host: Various
Frequency: Weekly
Average Show Length: 60 Minutes

Description
Love video games? IGN's Podcast Unlocked is your source for everything Xbox One. If you live and breathe Halo, Gears of War, Forza, and more, Podcast Unlocked has you covered. Tune in every week for the latest video game news for Xbox One and Xbox Live junkies around the globe.

PC Gamer
Host: Various
Frequency: Weekly
Average Show Length: 90 Minutes

Description
The official podcast of PC Gamer, the number one source of PC gaming news & reviews.

Jimquisition
Hosts: Jim Sterling, Laura Kate and Gavin Dunne
Frequency: Weekly
Average Show Length: 90 Minutes

Description
Audio home of The Jimquisition, featuring its lovely little podcast,
Podquisition - starring Jim Sterling, Laura Kate, and Gavin Dunne!

Making It
Hosts: Jimmy Diresta, Bob Clagett and David Picciuto
Frequency: Weekly
Average Show Length: 60 Minutes

Description
Making It is a weekly audio podcast hosted by Jimmy Diresta, Bob Clagett
and David Picciuto. Three different makers with different backgrounds
talking about creativity, design and making things with your bare hands.

The Angry Chicken
Hosts: Garrett Weinzierl and William "Dills" Gregory and Jocelyn Moffett
Frequency: Weekly
Average Show Length: 120 Minutes

Description
The Angry Chicken is a podcast that cracks 40 packs, throws down
a 1/1 chicken w/ a +5 Enrage, all the while keeping you up to date on
everything going on in the world of Hearthstone . Each week the latest
news, strategies, crazy game stories and your emails are covered. Garrett
Weinzierl (StarCast) and William "Dills" Gregory (The Instance), and Jocelyn
Moffett (The Gamers' Inn) together host The Angry Chicken.

The Comedy Button
Hosts: Brian Altano, Scott Bromley, Anthony Gallegos, Ryan Scott and Max
Scoville
Frequency: Weekly
Average Show Length: 60 Minutes

Description
What's going on, Internet!? Prepare for some of the most insane rambling
about everything from life, to sex, to what passes for 21st-century Internet
culture.

BeerSmith Home and Beer Brewing Podcast
Host: Dr. Brad Smith
Frequency: Weekly
Average Show Length: 60 Minutes

Description
The BeerSmith Home Brewing Show is a beer brewing podcast focused on how to brew beer, homebrewing techniques, and beer stories from top US and international brewers. In each episode we bring you an interview with guests assembled from around the world to talk about beer, craft beer and homebrew.

GOVERNMENT & ORGANIZATIONS

*2017 Government &
Organizations Top Pick*
SOFREP RADIO
Hosts: Brandon Webb,
Jack Murphy and Ian
Scotto
Frequency: Weekly
Average Show Length:
60 Minutes

The show is hosted by former Navy SEAL Sniper Instructor Brandon Webb, and Army Ranger/Green Beret Jack Murphy, alongside host and producer Ian Scotto. Welcome to uncensored, and politically incorrect "throat punch" content. Join us as we discuss anything from drones, foreign policy, modern warfare, terrorism, politics, and more. The show features guests from the Military, Intelligence, and Special Operations communities.

The Brookings Cafeteria
Host: Fred Drews
Frequency: Weekly
Average Show Length: 60 Minutes

Description:
Where Brookings experts discuss ideas about and solutions for the most pressing public policy challenges, both domestic and global.

U.S Supreme Court Oral Arguments
Host: Various
Frequency: Daily
Average Show Length: Various

Description:
Oral arguments before the Supreme Court of the United States, presented by Oyez, a multimedia judicial archive at the IllinoisTech Chicago-Kent College of Law.

No Jargon
Host: Various
Frequency: Weekly
Average Show Length: 30 Minutes

Description:
No Jargon, the Scholars Strategy Network's weekly podcast, presents interviews with top university scholars on the politics, policy problems, and social issues facing the nation. Powerful research, intriguing perspectives -- and no jargon.

Global Recon Podcast
Host: Various
Frequency: Weekly
Average Show Length: 60 Minutes

Description:
Welcome to the Global Recon Podcast! Tune in for a chance to hear from former SOF Operators, as well as military personnel from across the spectrum of military specialties.

Jay Sekulow Live Radio Show
Host: Jay Sekulow
Frequency: Daily
Average Show Length: 60 Minutes

Description:
Listen to our daily radio program, Jay Sekulow Live! for issues that matter most to you - national security, protecting America's families, and protecting human life. The reports are brought to you by the American Center for Law & Justice (ACLJ), a nonprofit organization specializing constitutional law and based in Washington, D.C.

RadioWest
Host: Doug Fabrizio
Frequency: Daily
Average Show Length: 60 Minutes

Description:
A radio conversation where people tell stories that explore the way the world works. Produced by KUER 90.1 in Salt Lake City and hosted by Doug Fabrizio.

Armed American Radio
Host: Mark Walters
Frequency: Daily
Average Show Length: 60 Minutes

Description:
Armed American Radio (AAR) is the official radio program of The United States Concealed Carry Association.

Intersections
Host: Adrianna Pita
Frequency: Weekly
Average Show Length: 60 Minutes

Description:
Economic recovery. Elections. Terrorism. Global poverty. Trade. Policy issues are complex and multifaceted. Want more than the 30-second soundbyte? Tune in to Intersections, a podcast from the Brookings Institution, where two experts delve into the varying angles of the complicated issues facing our nation and the world.

Chairborne Commandos
Host: Various
Frequency: Monthly
Average Show Length: 90 Minutes

Description:
Fasten your seatbelts! This is a military podcast and news talk radio show hosted by Veterans. If it goes fast, is highly explosive or dangerous, we talk about it on our show. We cover all branches of the US Armed Forces including Special Forces and top news stories from around the world.

Politics Politics Politics
Host: Justin Robert Young
Frequency: Daily
Average Show Length: 60 Minutes

Description:
Justin Robert Young announces his intention to dissect the run for the White House. Just think, while you been getting down and out about the liars and the dirty dirty cheats of the world you could have been getting down to this sick beat.

White House Speeches
Host: Various
Frequency: Daily
Average Show Length: Various

Description:
Keep up with all of the President's remarks, town halls, and press conferences in this comprehensive podcast. This feed will occasionally include remarks from other principals like the Vice President Biden and First Lady.

White House Press Briefings
Host: Various
Frequency: Daily
Average Show Length: Various

Description:
White House Press Briefings are conducted most weekdays from the James S. Brady Press Briefing Room in the West Wing. This feed will include occasional briefings by the President and other administration officials.

First Things Podcast
Host: Various
Frequency: Weekly
Average Show Length: 45 Minutes

Description:
First Things is published by The Institute on Religion and Public Life, an interreligious, nonpartisan research and education institute whose purpose is to advance a religiously informed public philosophy for the ordering of society.

This Week in Law
Hosts: Denise Howell, J. Michael Keyes and Emory Roane
Frequency: Weekly
Average Show Length: 45 Minutes

Description:
Join legal blogger (and trained attorney) Denise Howell along with J. Michael Keyes and Emory Roane as they discuss breaking issues in technology law, including patents, copyrights, and more. Records live every Friday.

The CSIS Podcast
Host: Colm Quinn
Frequency: Weekly
Average Show Length: 20 Minutes

Description:
A look at the week's news in foreign policy through the eyes of the experts at the Center for Strategic and International Studies (CSIS). CSIS is ranked the number one think tank for international affairs. CSIS provides strategic insights and bipartisan policy solutions.

Eagle Nation Podcast
Host: Blayne Smith
Frequency: Weekly
Average Show Length: 45 Minutes

Description:
Welcome to the Eagle Nation Podcast! We're excited to bring you a weekly dose of Eagle Fire through compelling discussions with inspiring guests, on topics that you care about. We'll explore veterans, community, nonprofits, fitness, and leadership.

Mentors for Military Podcast
Host: Various
Frequency: Weekly
Average Show Length: 45 Minutes

Description:
We are the BEST podcast for active duty military, veterans, or anyone wanting to be inspired or empowered! Our hosts are made up of a former US Army veteran turned corporate executive, two former US Army Special Forces soldiers (Green Beret) and one of the few female soldiers that was attached to the Rangers and Delta Force in Afghanistan. Our guests are corporate executives, Special Forces soldiers, active duty military, veterans, executive coaches, best-selling authors, keynote speakers, and from many other backgrounds.

Policing Matters
Host: Doug Wyllie and Jim Dudley
Frequency: Weekly
Average Show Length: 15 Minutes

Description:
Talking the beat with leaders and experts. PoliceOne is the world's most comprehensive and trusted online destination for law enforcement professionals, department decision-makers and industry experts. Founded in 1999, with more than 515,000 registered members representing more than 16,000 departments, PoliceOne effectively provides the law enforcement community with the information they need to protect their communities and come home safe after every shift.

The Shin Fujiyama Podcast
Host: Shin Fujiyama
Frequency: Weekly
Average Show Length: 15 Minutes

Description:
Shin Fujiyama is a CNN Hero and the Executive Director of Students Helping Honduras. He lives with 30 former street children in Honduras where he runs a school and international NGO. He lives on a wooden tree house built on a mango tree. In each episode Shin will be interviewing a proven social entrepreneur or NGO leader in the nonprofit or international development aid industry-- including several CNN Heroes and bestselling authors. They're going to deconstruct their journey to explain HOW they built up their organizations. They'll also tell us about their greatest failures, lessons, regrets, and behind-the-scenes realities. We'll talk about their tactics, philosophies, principles, tools, and motivations to give you inspiration and actionable advice.

Black Man With A Gun
Host: Kenn Blanchard
Frequency: Weekly
Average Show Length: 45 Minutes

Description:
Rev. Kenn Blanchard- a gun rights activist, author, trainer and professional speaker showcases the diversity of the gun culture with experts on hunting, gun rights, the justice system, American history, and self defense. It is done with humor and compassion for all people. He helps you "survive another week," by sharing positive people, products, and news with the wit

and humor of the gun rights activist since 2007. The show is not to incite but to inspire.

Federalist Society Event Audio
Host: Various
Frequency: Weekly
Average Show Length: 90 Minutes

Description:
The Federalist Society for Law and Public Policy Studies is a group of conservatives and libertarians interested in the current state of the legal order. It is founded on the principles that the state exists to preserve freedom, that the separation of governmental powers is central to our Constitution, and that it is emphatically the province and duty of the judiciary to say what the law is, not what it should be. This podcast feed contains audio files of Federalist Society panel discussions, debates, addresses, and other events related to law and public policy.

Federalist Society SCOTUScast
Host: Various
Frequency: Various
Average Show Length: 20 Minutes

Description:
SCOTUScast is a project of the Federalist Society for Law & Public Policy Studies. The Society a not for profit educational organization of conservative and libertarian law students, law professors, and lawyers, founded upon the principles that the state exists to preserve freedom, that the separation of governmental powers is central to our Constitution, and that it is emphatically the province and duty of the judiciary to say what the law is, not what it should be. This audio broadcast series provides expert commentary on U.S. Supreme Court cases as they are argued and issued. To supplement our scholars' analysis, we provide brief descriptions of the issues in the cases. The Federalist Society takes no position on particular legal or public policy issues; all expressions of opinion are those of the speaker. We hope these broadcasts, like all of our programming, will serve to stimulate discussion and further exchange regarding important current legal issues.

Black Agenda Radio
Host: Glen Ford and Nellie Bailey
Frequency: Weekly
Average Show Length: 60 Minutes

Description:
Hosts Glen Ford and Nellie Bailey, veterans of the Freedom Movement's many permutations and skilled communicators, host a weekly magazine designed to both inform and critique the global movement.

HEALTH

2017 Health Top Pick
SLEEP WITH ME
Host: Drew Ackerman
Frequency: Daily
Average Show Length:
60 Minutes

Are you up all night tossing and turning? Welcome to "Sleep With Me" The Podcast that Puts You to Sleep. We do it with a bedtime story. All you need to do is get in bed, turn out the lights and press play. Can't fall asleep? Mind racing at night? Worries keeping you awake? We are here to help! "Sleep With Me" is a groundbreaking podcast, that uses boredom superpowers to help you fall asleep. Kind of like a bedtime story for grownups, just interesting enough for you to forget your problems but boring enough to put you to sleep. So get in bed, press play and drift off into dreamland.

Good Life Project
Hosts: Jonathan Fields
Frequency: Daily
Average Show Length: 60 Minutes

Description:
Inspirational, unfiltered conversations and stories about finding meaning, happiness, purpose, inspiration, creativity, motivation, spirituality, love, confidence and success in life. From iconic world-shakers like Elizabeth Gilbert, Brene Brown, Sir Ken Robinson, Seth Godin and Gretchen Rubin to everyday people, every story matters.

Over It and On With It
Host: Christine Hassler
Frequency: Weekly
Average Show Length: 40 Minutes

Description:
Christine Hassler provides you with practical tools and spiritual principles to help you overcome whatever obstacles might be holding you back. Each episode, Christine coaches callers live on the air offering them inspiration and guidance to heal their past, change their present and create what they really want. Topics include: relationships, career, health, transitions, finances, life purpose, spirituality and whatever else callers have questions about. Christine coaches "regular people" on problems – and opportunities - we all face. It's a show that reminds you that you are not alone, while also teaching things you can implement in your own life.

Mental Illness Happy Hour
Host: Paul Gilmartin
Frequency: Weekly
Average Show Length: 40 Minutes

Description:
The Mental Illness Happy Hour is a weekly conversation between a guest and comedian/host Paul Gilmartin, focusing on the battles we have in our heads and the damage we feel. From medically diagnosed conditions to everyday compulsive negative thinking. This podcast is not a substitute for professional mental help, it's more like a waiting room that hopefully doesn't suck.

The School of Greatness
Host: Lewis Howes
Frequency: Daily
Average Show Length: 60 Minutes

Description:
Lewis Howes is a NYT bestselling author, lifestyle entrepreneur, former pro athlete and world record holder in football. The goal of the School of Greatness is to share inspiring stories from the most brilliant business minds, world class athletes and influential celebrities on the planet; to help you find out what makes great people great.

Starting Strength Channel
Host: Mark Rippetoe
Frequency: Weekly
Average Show Length: 30 Minutes

Description:
Starting Strength is the bestselling book on the most fundamental and effective approach to strength training ever written. Mark Rippetoe hosts The Starting Strength Channel where he discusses topics of interest, primarily to him, but perhaps also to you.

TEDTalks Health
Host: Various
Frequency: Weekly
Average Show Length: 15 Minutes

Description:
From way-new medical breakthroughs to smart daily health habits, doctors and researchers share their discoveries about medicine and well-being onstage at the TED conference, TEDx events and partner events around the world.

Happier
Host: Gretchen Rubin
Frequency: Daily
Average Show Length: 30 Minutes

Description:
Gretchen Rubin is HAPPIER, and she wants you to be happier too. The #1 bestselling author of The Happiness Project and Better Than Before gets more personal than ever as she brings her practical, manageable advice about happiness and good habits to this lively, thought-provoking podcast. Gretchen's co-host and guinea pig is her younger sister, Elizabeth Craft, a TV writer and producer living in Los Angeles, who (lovingly) refers to Gretchen as her happiness bully. Part of the Panoply Network.

Savage Lovecast
Host: Dan Savage
Frequency: Weekly
Average Show Length: 60 Minutes

Description:
Dan Savage, America's only advice columnist, answers your sex questions and yaps about politics.

Optimal Living Daily
Host: Justin Malik
Frequency: Daily
Average Show Length: 10 Minutes

Description:
I read you the best content on personal development, minimalism, productivity, and more, with author permission. Think of Optimal Living Daily as an audioblog or blogcast. :) Optimal Living Daily is a podcast created for those looking to improve their life one step at a time: lifelong learners, life hackers, and life optimizers. Justin Malik brings you the best content from blogs and other resources and reads it to you, so that you don't have to waste your time finding and reading blogs yourself--listen during your commute, workout, regular routines, or during your down time 7 days a week and improve your life one step at a time.

The Rich Roll Podcast
Host: Rich Roll
Frequency: Weekly
Average Show Length: 90 Minutes

Description:
A master-class in personal and professional development, ultra-athlete, wellness evangelist and bestselling author Rich Roll delves deep with the world's brightest and most thought provoking thought leaders to educate, inspire and empower you to unleash your best, most authentic self.

The Charged Life
Host: Brendon Burchard
Frequency: Weekly
Average Show Length: 20 Minutes

Description:
#1 New York Times bestselling author Brendon Burchard shares insights on motivation, success, high performance, and living a fully charged life.

Sex With Emily
Host: Emily Morse
Frequency: Daily
Average Show Length: 60 Minutes

Description:
Dr. Emily Morse shares her expertise on sex, relationships and everything in between!

The Minimalists
Hosts: Joshua Fields Millburn & Ryan Nicodemus
Frequency: Weekly
Average Show Length: 60 Minutes

Description:
Minimalism is the thing that gets us past the things so we can make room for life's most important things—which actually aren't things at all. At age 30, best friends Joshua Fields Millburn & Ryan Nicodemus walked away from their six-figure corporate careers, jettisoned most of their material possessions, and started focusing on what's truly important. In this podcast Joshua & Ryan, known to their millions of readers as "The Minimalists," discuss living a meaningful life with less stuff.

Barbell Shrugged
Hosts: Various
Frequency: Weekly
Average Show Length: 60 Minutes

Description:
New episode every Wednesday! Join the Barbell Shrugged crew in conversations about fitness, training, and frequent interviews w/ CrossFit Games athletes!

Bulletproof Radio

Host: Dave Asprey
Frequency: Weekly
Average Show Length: 60 Minutes

Description:
Bulletproof Executive Radio was born out of a fifteen-year single-minded crusade to upgrade the human being using every available technology. It distills the knowledge of world-class MDs, biochemists, Olympic nutritionists, meditation experts, and more than $250,000 spent on personal self-experiments. From private brain EEG facilities hidden in a Canadian forest to remote monasteries in Tibet, from Silicon Valley to the Andes, high tech entrepreneur Dave Asprey used hacking techniques and tried everything himself, obsessively focused on discovering: What are the simplest things you can do to be better at everything?

The Chalene Show

Host: Chalene Johnson
Frequency: Weekly
Average Show Length: 30 Minutes

Description:
Tips, resources, interviews and practical steps to help you improve energy, balance, organization, health, fitness, relationships, focus, faith and happiness. Each episode is designed to give you strategies and simple steps you can implement today to become a better, more balanced, happier version of yourself.

10% Happier

Host: Dan Harris
Frequency: Daily
Average Show Length: 45 Minutes

Description:
Dan Harris is a fidgety, skeptical ABC newsman who had a panic attack live on Good Morning America, which led him to something he always thought was ridiculous: meditation. He wrote the bestselling book, "10% Happier," started an app -- "10% Happier: Meditation for Fidgety Skeptics" -- and now, in this podcast, Dan talks with smart people about whether there's anything beyond 10%. Basically, here's what this podcast is obsessed with: Can you be an ambitious person and still strive for enlightenment (whatever that means)?

Operation Self Reset
Host: Jack Nawrocki
Frequency: Weekly
Average Show Length: 30 Minutes

Description:
Do you wish you were smarter, successful, happier, had more confidence, enjoyed life, had better relationships, better health, lived your dreams, took some more risks, didn't mind failing, had a positive attitude, loved more, helped more, and just become more of who you should be? Then I suggest you join the other 100,000+ subscribers to find out how to reset your life. This podcast is basically self-help 101. Changing your life is hard, but if you really want to change you can just by finding and pressing your reset button!

The Meditation Podcast
Producers: Jesse and Jeane Stern
Frequency: Monthly
Average Show Length: 30 Minutes

Description:
The Meditation Podcast is a free podcast designed to help you learn and benefit from meditation in your everyday life. The guided meditations contain audio technology that amplify slower brain waves to induce a relaxed and powerful altered meditative state of consciousness. Please use headphones, and do not listen while driving or operating machinery.

The Dr. Drew Podcast
Host: Dr. Drew Pinsky
Frequency: Weekly
Average Show Length: 60 Minutes

Description:
Dr. Drew Pinsky, board certified internist and addiction medicine specialist, takes listener calls and talks to experts on a variety of topics relating to health, relationships, sex and drug addiction.

Ben Greenfield Fitness
Host: Ben Greenfield
Frequency: Weekly
Average Show Length: 60 Minutes

Description:
Free exercise, nutrition, weight loss, triathlon and wellness advice from BenGreenfieldFitness.com! Tune in to the latest health, fitness and multi-sport research, non run-of-the-mill interviews with exercise and medicine professionals, and new cutting-edge content from the top personal trainer and wellness coach in the nation.

Fat-Burning Man
Host: Abel James
Frequency: Weekly
Average Show Length: 60 Minutes

Description:
Abel James answers your questions and interviews leaders in alternative health, Paleo, and natural wellness to share secrets about losing fat, building muscle, and upgrading your health. Winner of 4 awards and #1 in Health in 8+ countries. Come join the fun!

Fitness Confidential
Hosts: Vinnie Tortorich and Anna Vocino
Frequency: Daily
Average Show Length: 60 Minutes

Description:
Hollywood Celebrity Trainer Vinnie Tortorich and his co-host Anna Vocino nail down the skinny about everything health, diet, and fitness. Get fit. Get inspired. Get entertained.

The Model Health Show
Host: Shawn Stevenson
Frequency: Weekly
Average Show Length: 60 Minutes

Description:
The Model Health Show is a fun, entertaining, and enlightening look at health and fitness. No subject is off limits here! World-renown author and nutritionist Shawn Stevenson breaks down complex health issues and makes them easy to understand and overcome. Whether it's weight

loss, chronic fatigue, heart disease, diet, exercise, sex, hormones, sleep problems, or countless other health topics, the insights you get here will help you transform your health and live your best life ever.

Finding Mastery
Host: Michael Gervais
Frequency: Weekly
Average Show Length: 60 Minutes

Description:
Dr. Michael Gervais is fascinated by the psychology of high performance, in rugged environments. Throughout the past 15 years, Michael has been in the trenches with some of the best performers in the world — some who shift how we conceive what's possible — others who have pushed their own boundaries — ranging from hall of fame athletes to action sport game-changers, entrepreneurs, Mixed Martial Artists, to musicians who influence the rhythm of the world. He's excited to share the many paths toward mastery and provide very applied practices that we can all use to be and do more in our time together.

Food Psych
Host: Christy Harrison
Frequency: Weekly
Average Show Length: 60 Minutes

Description:
Helping people make peace with food since 2013. Registered Dietitian Nutritionist and Certified Intuitive Eating Counselor Christy Harrison, MPH, RD, CDN talks with guests about their relationships with food, body image, eating disorders, weight and size acceptance, non-diet nutrition, exercise, self-compassion and self-care--all from a body-positive, Health at Every Size perspective. Along the way, Christy shares her own journey from disordered eater and dieter to food writer and anti-diet dietitian, and offers tips to help you accept your body and let go of guilt about food.

Daily Meditation Podcast
Host: Mary Meckley
Frequency: Daily
Average Show Length: 15 Minutes

Description:
A Library of Meditations at Your Finger Tips: Join meditation coach, Mary Meckley, for daily meditation inspiration as she answers your questions and guides you on the journey of establishing a daily meditation ritual. Each week you're introduced to a brand new meditation theme to keep your meditations dynamic. Mary provides guidance as you sit down to meditate with her each day. She shows you how to make meditation a natural part of your day... not something that interrupts your day.

Inspiration Living
Host: Various
Frequency: Daily
Average Show Length: 20 Minutes

Description:
The Inspirational Living podcast offers motivational broadcasts for the mind, body, and spirit. Master the art of living a life of success, happiness, creativity, and beauty. Each podcast is edited & adapted from the books and essays of classic inspirational writers, such as Kahlil Gibran, Ralph Waldo Emerson, Helen Keller, Oscar Wilde, James Allen, Ella Wheeler Wilcox, Orison Swett Marden, Neville Goddard, and Henry David Thoreau, as well as self-development authors who have largely been lost to history but deserve to be heard again and enjoyed.

The Secret To Success
Host: Eric Thomas PhD
Frequency: Weekly
Average Show Length: 60 Minutes

Description:
From homeless, high school dropout to Entrepreneur, C.E.O. and Ph.D.! Hear first hand how Eric was able to defy the odds, and single-handedly break the negative generational cycles that plagued his family for decades. Join the conversation with ET and co-host Carlas Quinney Jr. and learn how you too can create the life you deserve.

The 5 AM Miracle
Host: Jeff Sanders
Frequency: Weekly
Average Show Length: 45 Minutes

Description:
The 5 AM Miracle is a weekly podcast dedicated to dominating your day before breakfast. My goal is to help you bounce out of bed with enthusiasm, create powerful lifelong habits, and tackle your grandest goals with extraordinary energy.

Revolution Health Radio
Host: Chris Hessler
Frequency: Weekly
Average Show Length: 50 Minutes

Description:
Revolution Health Radio debunks mainstream myths on nutrition and health and delivers cutting-edge, yet practical information on how to prevent and reverse disease naturally.

The Unbeatable Mind Podcast
Host: Mark Divine
Frequency: Weekly
Average Show Length: 50 Minutes

Description:
Retired Navy SEAL Commander Mark Divine and his SEALFIT Coaching team take on guests with subject matters that follow along with Mark's 5 mountain training path of developing your Mental, Physical, Emotional, Intuitive, and Kokoro (Heart) self.

20 Min. Yoga Sessions
Host: Various
Frequency: Weekly
Average Show Length: 50 Minutes

Description:
YogaDownload.com brings you 20 minute yoga sessions to help you relax, become more centered, and bring balance to your body, mind and soul. Choose from a wide-variety of yoga styles and themes perfect for any mood or day of the week.

The Overwhelmed Brain
Host: Paul Colaianni
Frequency: Weekly
Average Show Length: 60 Minutes

Description:
If you've been struggling with anxiety, depression, fears, obsession, panic, or any relationship, marriage or family issues, or just want less stress and more happiness, this show will empower you to honor yourself and make decisions that are right for you. Mindfulness, compassion and being in the present moment are only components of a bigger picture. Honoring yourself and living authentically, along with strengthening your emotional intelligence are a few of the keys to an empowered life. If you're annoyed with affirmations and tired of being told to "think positively!", this is the show that leaves out the fluff and gives you practical, down to earth steps to help you create the life you want.

Earn Your Happy Podcast
Host: Lori Harder
Frequency: Weekly
Average Show Length: 60 Minutes

Description:
Get all the inside secrets and tools you need to help you bust through your fears, connect to your soul and get focused and clear so you can elevate your life, business and relationships... Listen in as Lori Harder, founder of the Bliss Project, 3X time fitness world champion, fitness expert and cover model, turned self love junkie - lifestyle entrepreneur and author digs in shares the goods! Each episode is designed to give you the tools, ideas, and inspiration to take action in your life. Tune in for an inspirational guest, a story or a "quickie" of motivation to get you out of a funk or blast you even further on your rockstar journey!

Order of Man
Host: Ryan Michler
Frequency: Weekly
Average Show Length: 40 Minutes

Description:
Become more of the man you were meant to be. Order of Man is for motivated and ambitious men who want to become better in every area of their lives from defining their purpose, obtaining self-mastery, building relationships, growing as a leader, and mastering business and finances.

Each week, Ryan Michler has real, unscripted conversations with the world's most successful men.

The Jillian Michaels Show
Host: Jillian Michaels
Frequency: Weekly
Average Show Length: 60 Minutes

Description:
Jillian Michaels, America's Health and Wellness guru, brings you the Jillian Michaels Show. An entertaining, inspirational, informative show that gives you tools to find health and happiness in all areas of your life.

Kiss Me Quick's Erotica
Host: Rose Caraway
Frequency: Weekly
Average Show Length: 45 Minutes

Description:
Rose Caraway entices listeners with alluring, erotic, tales in "The Kiss-Me-Quick's" Erotica Podcast. This sexy and adventurous show will simultaneously provoke the mind and arouse the senses. Prepare to experience sex with a range of emotions as Rose Caraway regales you with her astonishing tales that will delight, thrill, and at times horrify. -This show contains fictional sexual content: Consider yourself warned.

Sex Nerd Sandra
Host: Sandra Daugherty
Frequency: Weekly
Average Show Length: 60 Minutes

Description:
Curious about the naughty side of life? Come giggle with Sandra at the cuddly side of the sex pool! Exploring fascinating topics & perspectives on sex & love, join sexuality educator Sandra Daugherty & special guests for a loving laugh at the fundamentals of human nature.

The Livin' La Vida Low-Carb Show
Host: Jimmy Moore
Frequency: Daily
Average Show Length: 60 Minutes

Description:
On Mondays, Tuesdays and Wednesdays, low-carb blogger Jimmy Moore presents interviews with the movers and shakers in the world of Low-Carb/Paleo science, medicine and living. We're here to help, encourage, inspire, motivate and rattle some chains.

No Meat Athlete
Host: Matt Frazier
Frequency: Weekly
Average Show Length: 60 Minutes

Description:
Vegan and vegetarian nutrition, running and training tips, and healthy lifestyle and habit change with well-known guests like Rich Roll, Brendan Brazier, Heather Crosby, Leo Babauta, Rip Esselstyn, Nicole Antoinette, make for an entertaining, informative, no-preach listen.

The Paleo Solution
Host: Robb Wolf
Frequency: Weekly
Average Show Length: 60 Minutes

Description:
A free, weekly podcast where Robb answers your questions about Paleo nutrition, intermittent fasting, training, fitness, and more.

Balanced Bites
Hosts: Diane Sanfilippo and Liz Wolfe
Frequency: Weekly
Average Show Length: 60 Minutes

Description:
Diane is the New York Times bestselling author of "Practical Paleo" and "The 21-Day Sugar Detox" and is a Certified Nutrition Consultant. Liz is the bestselling author of "Eat the Yolks" and "The Purely Primal Skincare Guide" and a Nutritional Therapy Practitioner. Each week, Diane and Liz dish on current topics in health, nutrition, and the Paleosphere as well as provide insights in response to listener questions - all with their signature

wit and a healthy dose of joking around that'll make you feel like you're spending an hour with two of your best girlfriends each week.

Total Human Optimization
Hosts: Aubrey Marcus and Orlando Rios
Frequency: Weekly
Average Show Length: 60 Minutes

Description:
Our mission is to inspire peak performance through a combination of unique products and actionable information. Combining bleeding-edge science, earth-grown nutrients, and time-tested strategies from top athletes and medical professionals, we are dedicated to providing our listeners with supplements, foods, and fitness equipment aimed at helping people achieve a new level of well-being we call Total Human Optimization.

The Paleo Women Podcast
Hosts: Stefani Ruper and Noelle Tarr
Frequency: Weekly
Average Show Length: 60 Minutes

Description:
Authentic, unfiltered conversations about health, fitness, nutrition, mindset, and body image with Noelle Tarr, Nutritional Therapy Practitioner and Certified Personal Trainer, and Stefani Ruper, author of the best-selling book Sexy By Nature. Expect real talk, moderately amusing banter, and empowering advice for women, from women.

FoundMyFitness
Host: Rhonda Patrick, PhD
Frequency: Weekly
Average Show Length: 60 Minutes

Description:
Promoting strategies to increase healthspan, well-being, cognitive and physical performance through deeper understandings of biology.

Primal Blueprint
Host: Mark Sisson
Frequency: Daily
Average Show Length: 60 Minutes

Description:
On how to be healthy, strong, fit, happy and productive with the least amount of pain, suffering and sacrifice as possible. Featuring Primal Blueprint author Mark Sisson (marksdailyapple.com) and other guests from the ancestral health community.

Spinning Logic
Host: Jason Havey
Frequency: Weekly
Average Show Length: 90 Minutes

Description:
The goal of Spinning Logic is to thread together the unique stories of unique guests and to celebrate the vast array of people that represent humankind.

KIDS & FAMILY

2017 Kids & Family
Top Pick
BRAINS ON!
Host: Molly Bloom
Frequency: Weekly
Average Show Length:
20 Minutes

Brains On is a science podcast for curious kids and adults from MPR News and KPCC. Co-hosted each week by kid scientists and reporters from public radio, we ask questions ranging from the science behind sneezing to how to translate the purr of cats, and go wherever the answers take us.

The Casey Crew
Host: DJ Envy and Gia Casey
Frequency: Weekly
Average Show Length: 60 Minutes

Description:
DJ and radio host DJ Envy and his wife Gia Casey will explore the good, bad, ugly and beauty of relationships and family. Join them every week as they let you in on past experiences, give advice, talk to celebrity couples and give you two sides to every situation.

Respectful Parenting: Janet Lansbury Unruffled
Host: DJ Envy and Gia Casey
Frequency: Weekly
Average Show Length: 20 Minutes

Description:
Each episode addresses a reader's parenting issue through the lens of Janet's respectful parenting philosophy. Janet is a respected parenting adviser, author, and guest lecturer whose website (JanetLansbury.com) is visited by millions of readers annually. Her work informs, inspires, and supports caregivers of infants and toddlers across the globe, helping to create relationships of respect, trust, and love.

Storynory
Host: Natasha Gostwick
Frequency: Weekly
Average Show Length: 20 Minutes

Description:
Storynory brings you an audio story every week. Each one is beautifully read by Natasha and friends. Let Natasha's voice beguile you with classic fairy tales, new children's stories, poems, myths, adventures and romance.

God Centered Mom
Host: Heather MacFadyen
Frequency: Weekly
Average Show Length: 45 Minutes

Description:
LIfe is messy. Some days (some hours) are harder than others. Heather MacFadyen, mother of four boys, understands the wild ride. In this podcast she interviews guests about staying God-centered in a shaky mom world. Hearing vulnerable moments and examples of God's faithfulness in the past, helps you, the listener, build firm faith foundations for the future. Reminding us of our position--centered in God's presence and love.

Read-Aloud Revival
Host: Sarah Mackenzie
Frequency: Weekly
Average Show Length: 45 Minutes

Description:
The Read-Aloud Revival Podcast is the place to get the inspiration and resources you need to read aloud to your kids. Get motivated and encouraged to build your family culture around books! The podcast is a collection of inspiring and informative interviews to help parents, homeschoolers, and teachers make reading aloud a central part of family life. Reading aloud is more than just a literary education- it's a framework for family culture.

Sesame Street
Host: Various
Frequency: Weekly
Average Show Length: 5 Minutes

Description:
Download and subscribe to the Sesame Street video podcast featuring the furry and loveable Muppets of Sesame Street. Sing songs with Elmo, Abby, Cookie Monster and Grover. Learn about friendship, patience and sharing with Bert and Ernie. Celebrate sunny days with all of your favorite Muppets with new episodes every Monday!

Focus on Marriage
Host: Various
Frequency: Weekly
Average Show Length: 10 Minutes

Description:
Timeless wisdom from Focus on the Family that will challenge and encourage you in your marriage.

The Official Adventures in Odyssey
Host: Various
Frequency: Weekly
Average Show Length: 20 Minutes

Description:
Created for children ages 8-12 (but loved by listeners of all ages), Adventures in Odyssey is a 30-minute drama that combines the faith lessons parents appreciate with characters and stories that kids love! The official podcast gives behind-the-scenes information on the show, gives deleted scenes and answers fan questions.

ONE Extraordinary Marriage Show
Hosts: Tony and Alisa DiLorenzo
Frequency: Weekly
Average Show Length: 30 Minutes

Description:
Is your marriage everything that you want it to be? Are you ready to make a change? Join Tony and Alisa DiLorenzo to create a strong marriage so you can have mind-blowing intimacy inside and outside the bedroom. Marriage is not always easy but it's so worth it.

The Birth Hour
Host: Bryn Huntpalmer
Frequency: Weekly
Average Show Length: 45 Minutes

Description:
Bryn Huntpalmer provides a space for pregnant women to learn from pregnancy & birth stories of all types.

Parenting Great Kids
Host: Dr. Meg Meeker
Frequency: Weekly
Average Show Length: 45 Minutes

Description:
Parents are trying to navigate children through a world they themselves don't often understand. America's Mom, Dr. Meg Meeker, the country's trusted authority on parenting, teens, & children's health, offers practical insights to help parents simplify. The pediatrician, mother, & best selling author engages with experts & parents to take on relevant issues, answer real questions, & provide simple hope & encouragement to every parent.

Focus on Parenting
Host: Various
Frequency: Weekly
Average Show Length: 10 Minutes

Description:
Need help with raising your kids? Focus on the Family provides tried and true parenting advice to help your children thrive.

Tumble Science Podcast for Kids
Hosts: Lindsay Patterson and Marshall Escamilla
Frequency: Weekly
Average Show Length: 20 Minutes

Description:
Exploring stories of science discovery. Tumble is a science podcast created to be enjoyed by the entire family. Hosted & produced by Lindsay Patterson (science journalist) & Marshall Escamilla (teacher).

Marriage More
Hosts: Jeff Rose and Mandy Rose
Frequency: Weekly
Average Show Length: 30 Minutes

Description:
Jeff and Mandy Rose have been married for over a decade and they've been through it all. Their podcast is designed to help couples make their marriage more by going through various Love Challenges.

FamilyLife Today
Host: Dennis Rainey
Frequency: Daily
Average Show Length: 30 Minutes

Description:
FamilyLife Today® is a daily 25 to 30 minute podcast that provides practical, biblical tools to address the issues affecting your family in a format that is conversational in nature. At the core of every program is motivation, encouragement, and help.

Story Time
Narrator: Rob Griffiths
Frequency: Weekly
Average Show Length: 10 Minutes

Description:
Do your children like listening to bedtime stories? Story Time has lots of great stories for everyone to listen to. Each story is usually less than 20 minutes long, hopefully just long enough to keep your toddler, preschoolers, and little ones engaged. Story Time is a free fortnightly audiobook podcast for children ages 2-12. Narrated by Rob Griffiths

The Mighty Mommy
Host: Cheryl Butler
Frequency: Weekly
Average Show Length: 10 Minutes

Description:
Whether you're dealing with baby colic, your toddler's tantrums, your tween's moods, or your teen's college applications, Mighty Mommy has parenting tips to help make your family life easier and much more fun. As the mother of 8 kids, Cheryl Butler has seen it all - and survived.

At Home With Sally
Host: Sally Clarkson
Frequency: Weekly
Average Show Length: 40 Minutes

Description:
Home is the place where the whispers of God's love are heard regularly, the touch of His hands is given intentionally throughout the day, the words of His encouragement and affirmation pointed to lay the foundation of loving relationships where a woman conducts the beauty of this life within its walls.

Slate's Mom & Dad Are Fighting
Hosts: Allison Benedikt and Dan Kois
Frequency: Weekly
Average Show Length: 45 Minutes

Description:
Slate editors Allison Benedikt and Dan Kois review and debate the latest parenting news, and try to stay civil. Part of the Panoply Network.

Sparkle Stories
Host: David Sewell McCan
Frequency: Weekly
Average Show Length: 45 Minutes

Description:
Sparkle Stories produces original audio stories for families around the world. Each week on the Sparkle Stories Podcast, we'll be sharing a Free Story from one of our Original Story Series!

The Anna and Susannah Show
Hosts: Anna Thomas and Susannah Lewis
Frequency: Weekly
Average Show Length: 60 Minutes

Description:
Funny women, Anna of HaHas for HooHas and Susannah of Whoa Susannah, share funny stories at our own expense. And maybe at the expense of our husbands. And kids. Whatever.

The Good Dad Project
Host: Larry Hagner
Frequency: Weekly
Average Show Length: 30 Minutes

Description:
The Good Dad Project is a movement. It is a strong community of Fathers who all share a set of values. Larry Hagner, founder of the Good Dad Project, breaks down common challenges of fatherhood, makes them easy to understand, and overcome. Tackling the world of Fatherhood can be a daunting task when we try to do it alone. The mission of The Good Dad Project is to help you become the best, strongest, and happiest version of yourself so that you can help guide your kids to the best version of themselves. Simple as that.

Mom Struggling Well
Host: Emily Thomas
Frequency: Weekly
Average Show Length: 45 Minutes

Description:
Join me each week as I chat with a friend about a challenge they've had and how they struggled WELL through it. Don't worry though. It's not ALL about kids OR sadness. It's funny too. Promise. So, I dare you to listen. And subscribe. And tell everyone you know.

MouseChat.net
Hosts: Various
Frequency: Weekly
Average Show Length: 50 Minutes

Description:
Disney Radio Show - Disney World Trip Planning, Disney World Events, and News with a fun family point of view. Join us each week on the MouseChat. net Podcast as we discuss the latest Disney news from the parks and resorts all around Disney World. For Disney Fans by Disney Fans.

The Birthful Podcast
Hosts: Various
Frequency: Weekly
Average Show Length: 60 Minutes

Description:
Women get bombarded with all sorts of advice on maternity: a lot of it unsolicited, and often outdated or just plain incorrect. In the Birthful Podcast, Adriana Lozada talks with pregnancy, birth and postpartum experts to distill that information down to the relevant stuff. Think of us as your own specialized team of birth pros! We know that being pregnant can be tough. That being a mom can be hard. That having a baby can be exhausting. And we hope to make it easier by giving you tried and tested tips and tools that you can use. From "laid-back" breastfeeding to safer bed-sharing, circumcision to VBACs, we'll give you well-researched, evidence-based information so YOU can make the choices that best fit your family.

How To Be A Girl
Host: Marlo Mack
Frequency: Monthly
Average Show Length: 30 Minutes

Description:
How to Be a Girl is an audio podcast I produce about life with my six-year-old transgender daughter. It stars the two of us -- a single mom and a six-year-old "girl with a penis" -- as we attempt together to sort out just what it means to be a girl.

Pregnancy Podcast
Host: Vanessa Merten
Frequency: Weekly
Average Show Length: 20 Minutes

Description:
Pregnancy, Birth, Being a New Parent made easy! The Pregnancy Podcast is a podcast all about navigating the crazy awesomeness that is pregnancy, birth, and being a new parent! Vanessa Merten provides info that goes way beyond the typical "pregnancy instruction manual" by sharing all of the pros and cons, different perspectives, the latest research, and expert guests here and there — all so you decide what the best option is for YOU and feel confident about your decisions while you are pregnant and beyond. The Pregnancy Podcast covers everything from pregnancy,

prenatal care, labor, natural birth, breast feeding, newborns, and being a new parent. The Pregnancy Podcast is a resource to help you make informed decisions about your pregnancy and your baby. Rest assured, you'll find the real solutions that are in line with your family and your lifestyle.

Enjoying Life On A Budget Podcast
Host: Mark Greutman and Lauren Greutman
Frequency: Weekly
Average Show Length: 20 Minutes

Description:
Here on the Enjoying Life on a Budget Podcast we share simple, easy ways to take back control of your money, live within your means, and create the simpler happier life we've always dreamed of. Mark and Lauren Greutman - authors of the website iamthatlady.com share their money management, debt reduction, and simple easy recipes for being financially wise.

The Homemaking Foundations Podcast
Host: Jami Balmet
Frequency: Weekly
Average Show Length: 30 Minutes

Description:
The Homemaking Foundations podcast exists to give you the tools, inspiration, and encouragement that you need to craft a Gospel-Centered Home! Join Jami, author behind YoungWifesGuide.com, as we explore various aspects of homemaking including Biblical womanhood, marriage, healthy living, organizing, cooking, and so much more! If you feel like your home is out of control - or if you ever feel overwhelmed in your role as homemaker - then join Jami each week as she interviews other homemakers and provides Gospel-Centered encouragement for bringing Glory to God every day within our homes.

The Homemaking Foundations Podcast
Hosts: Cathy Cassani Adams and Todd Adams
Frequency: Weekly
Average Show Length: 60 Minutes

Description:
Zen Parenting is a weekly online radio discussion between a spiritual and emotional mom (Cathy Cassani Adams) and a logical and practical dad

(Todd Adams). Anyone else living a life like that?

Parenting on Purpose
Hosts: Bob Barnes and Torrey Roberts
Frequency: Daily
Average Show Length: 15 Minutes

Description:
Parenting On Purpose is a resource for parents dealing with everyday parenting issues.

Marriage Is Funny
Hosts: Jessie Artigue and Gerard Brown
Frequency: Weekly
Average Show Length: 50 Minutes

Description:
These are honest conversations from a married couple who is trying to figure it out like everybody else. The best recipe for a healthy marriage is the right mix of love + laughter, and we believe that talking things out and tight bear hugs fix [almost] everything. Join us on the journey and we'll show you that there is humor in every mess.

For Crying Out Loud
Hosts: Lynette Carolla and Stefanie Wilder-Taylor
Frequency: Weekly
Average Show Length: 60 Minutes

Description:
TV executive Lynette Carolla, wife of comedian Adam, along with comedy writer and best-selling parenting author of Sippy Cups are Not For Chardonnay - Stefanie Wilder-Taylor are two mothers of twins breaking it down parenting style. In this raucous hour of conversations they cover a range of topics from their marriages and kids, to the pros and cons of ferberizing to which one of the Real Housewives have had too much filler (all of them). The format is informative, loose and most of all entertaining. A wide variety of guests show up such as friends of The Adam Carolla show, (David Alan Grier, Greg Fitzsimmons, Teresa Strasser, the lovable Dr. Bruce) as well as big names in the parenting biz to personal friends and anyone that they find interesting. This hour will feel like you're hanging with your best girl friends. Lynette and Stefanie are honest, silly and sometimes become vulnerable as they discuss their own experiences as wife and mom.

MUSIC

ALL SONGS CONSIDERED
Hosts: Bob Boilen and Rob Hilton
Frequency: Daily
Average Show Length: 40 Minutes

Hosts Bob Boilen and Robin Hilton spin new music from emerging bands and musical icons.

Drink Champs
Hosts: N.O.R.E and DJ EFN
Frequency: Weekly
Average Show Length: 90 Minutes

Description:
Legendary Queens rapper and one half of Capone-n-Noreaga N.O.R.E. alongside Miami hip-hop pioneer DJ EFN come together as the Drink Champs. Listen in as N.O.R.E., DJ EFN and special guests talk over some drinks and discuss everything from current events to old school stories. Nothing is sacred when talking with the Drink Champs so this show is not for the easily offended!

Tiny Desk Concerts
Host: Bob Boilen
Frequency: Weekly
Average Show Length: 20 Minutes

Description:
Tiny Desk Concerts from NPR Music feature your favorite musicians performing at All Songs Considered host Bob Boilen's desk in the NPR office. Hear Wilco, Adele, Passion Pit, Tinariwen, Miguel, The xx and many more. This is the audio version of the podcast.

The Combat Jack Show
Host: Combat Jack
Frequency: Weekly
Average Show Length: 20 Minutes

Description:
The undisputed #1 HipHop podcast, the Combat Jack Show features interviews with HipHop icons & the most in-depth conversations about music, news, culture & race. Listen to Russell Simmons, Chuck D, Damon Dash, Rza, Scarface, D-Nice and more share personal stories and talk exclusively about their journeys, philosophies and viewpoints.

I'll Name This Podcast Later
Host: Joe Budden
Frequency: Weekly
Average Show Length: 60 Minutes

Description:
Joe Budden and his friend Rory sit down every week to discuss life, music, sex, and more. Tune in and follow along the crazy adventures of these very random friends.

Above & Beyond: Group Therapy
Host: Various
Frequency: Weekly
Average Show Length: 60 Minutes

Description:
Group Therapy is the weekly radio show from Above & Beyond also known as ABGT

The Talkhouse Music Podcast
Host: Various
Frequency: Weekly
Average Show Length: 60 Minutes

Description:
Smart, notable musicians from all genres and generations writing about current releases. Join the conversation! Naturally, no one knows more about music than musicians. They talk about their own work all the time, but they rarely get to talk about other people's music. That's what the Talkhouse is all about: smart, distinguished musicians from all genres and generations writing about the latest releases

Clublife
Host: DJ Tiësto
Frequency: Weekly
Average Show Length: 60 Minutes

Description:
Subscribe to Clublife by Tiësto for an hour of the best club tracks from around the world with your favorite DJ.

Snoop Dogg's GGN Podcast
Host: Snoop Dogg
Frequency: Monthly
Average Show Length: 30 Minutes

Description:
Wake and bake cuz! Down to smoke one with your big homie Snoop Dogg? Well, here I is and here's your shot neffew. Get up close and personal with me – the one and only Snoop Dogg each week on my official GGN podcast. This podcast right here is hosted by none other than me...yours truly...music legend and pop culture icon... Snoop D-O-double G ya dig?!? This is nuthin but a smoked out session rolled tightly into podcast form that features me choppin' game with and doin' full-length interviews with a who's who from the entertainment world. Listen to some funny ass comedic tales or me bustin' some off tha cuff freestyles. Man, me and my guests speak on everything related to popular culture. No one does uncensored and uncut quite like ya boy Big Snoop...aka Finding Nemo... aka Nemo Hoes. And now I'm inviting you to blaze one up with us and jump on in.

Rap Radar
Hosts: Elliot Wilson and Brian "B.Dot" Miller
Frequency: Weekly
Average Show Length: 60 Minutes

Description:
Hip hop's premier website connects with our culture's most important voices. Hosted by Elliot Wilson and Brian "B.Dot" Miller.

KEXP Song of the Day
Host: Various
Frequency: Daily
Average Show Length: 5 Minutes

Description:
KEXP's Song of the Day podcast features exclusive in-studio performances, unreleased songs, and recordings from independent musicians that KEXP thinks listeners should hear along with songs from more well-known artists.

A State of Trance
Host: Armin van Buuren
Frequency: Weekly
Average Show Length: 20 Minutes

Description:
Every week, Armin selects his favourite tunes of the A State of Trance radio show and puts them into his official Podcast. Expect a blend of the hottest in trance and progressive. Enjoy!

Dissect
Host: Various
Frequency: Weekly
Average Show Length: 30 Minutes

Description:
Dissect is a serialized music podcast that breaks long form musical analysis into short, digestible episodes. Season 1 is dedicated entirely to To Pimp a Butterfly by Kendrick Lamar. Over nearly 20 episodes, we'll dissect this Grammy-award winning record measure-by-measure, word-by-word, until we reach a complete understanding of this modern masterpiece.

Song Exploder
Host: Hrishikesh Hirway
Frequency: Weekly
Average Show Length: 15 Minutes

Description:
A podcast where musicians take apart their songs, and piece by piece, tell the story of how they were made.

Speed Dial
Hosts: Doreen St-Felix and Ira Midson III
Frequency: Weekly
Average Show Length: 15 Minutes

Description:
Ira and Doreen look at music, film, and celebrity through the lens of Ira and Doreen.

Hardwell On Air Official Podcast
Host: Hardwell
Frequency: Weekly
Average Show Length: 60 Minutes

Description:
"Hardwell On Air" will give everyone's weekend that extra boost, by bringing that trendsetting and original Hardwell sound! Next to Hardwell's latest floorfillers, the show gives a platform to new DJ talent with the item " Demo of the Week". Be sure to tune in!

Music Podcast
Hosts: Jon Pareles, Jon Caramanica and Nate Chinen
Frequency: Weekly
Average Show Length: 60 Minutes

Description:
New York Times music critics Jon Pareles, Jon Caramanica and Nate Chinen talk each week about the latest pop music news, the top songs, the best albums, the biggest stars — and the up and coming stars you haven't heard of yet.

Live In Concert
Host: Various
Frequency: Various
Average Show Length: 60 Minutes

Description:
Hear live shows from Spiritualized, Andrew Bird, Wilco, Bon Iver, Alabama Shakes, Beirut and many more. Recorded by NPR Music at venues and festivals across the country.

Monstercat Podcast
Host: Various
Frequency: Weekly
Average Show Length: 60 Minutes

Description:
The #MonstercatPodcast is a weekly radio show featuring 1 hour of dance music. Showcasing multiple genres and styles, let us take you on a journey.

Nice Hair with The Chainsmokers
Host: The Chainsmokers
Frequency: Monthly
Average Show Length: 60 Minutes

Description:
The Chainsmokers' sharp wit and self deprecating humor, paired with their diverse taste in music make this one of the most entertaining and enjoyable shows on Sirius. Make sure you tune in as the duo regularly premiere new material from themselves and industry friends and do other weird stuff. Nice Hair owns all permissions and necessary licensing to play the music on their show.

Alt.Latino
Hosts: Felix Contreras and Jasmine Garsd
Frequency: Weekly
Average Show Length: 45 Minutes

Description:
A voyage across the world in search of the best new Rock en Espanol and Latin Alternative music releases. Co-hosts Felix Contreras and Jasmine Garsd also pay tribute to the pioneers of the genre.

Sound Opinions
Hosts: Jim DeRogatis and Greg Kot
Frequency: Weekly
Average Show Length: 60 Minutes

Description:
Sound Opinions is the World's only rock and roll talkshow. Hosted by Jim DeRogatis of WBEZ and Greg Kot of the Chicago Tribune. Each week Jim and Greg bring you the latest music news and reviews. Plus tune in to hear exclusive interviews and performances. Sound Opinions is a production of WBEZ Chicago and distributed by PRX. Updated weekly.

Juan Epstein
Host: Peter Rosenberg
Frequency: Weekly
Average Show Length: 60 Minutes

Description:
Cipha Sounds and Peter Rosenberg's 'Juan Epstein' is the longest
running and most beloved hip hop nerdcast on the planet. Based in the
legendary Hot 97 studios, Ciph and Rosenberg go in depth on Hip Hop
with EVERYONE. They ask the questions that only TRUE nerdy fans can
ask. Past guests include Jay-Z, Eminem, Aziz Ansari, Big Daddy Kane,
Ghostface, Diamond D, Redman, Patrice O'neal, and many more! Hundreds
of hours of Hip Hop gold.

Spinnin' Sessions
Host: Various
Frequency: Weekly
Average Show Length: 60 Minutes

Description:
Spinnin' Records proudly presents its weekly radio show: Spinnin'
Sessions. Besides providing you with the most upfront dance floor tracks
of the moment, Spinnin Sessions will also welcome a weekly guest DJ for a
special 30 minute mix. Enjoy!

Mountain Stage
Host: Larry Groce
Frequency: Weekly
Average Show Length: 60 Minutes

Description:
For over 30 years, Mountain Stage has been the home of live music
on public radio. Produced by West Virginia Public Broadcasting, each
two-hour episode features performances from seasoned legends and
emerging stars in genres ranging from folk, blues, and country; to indie
rock, pop, world music, alternative, and beyond.

Irish and Celtic Music Podcast
Host: Marc Gunn
Frequency: Weekly
Average Show Length: 60 Minutes

Description:
The Irish & Celtic Music Podcast is an award-winning free Celtic radio show of independent Irish & Celtic music. The show won "Best Podsafe Music" in 2009 and 2010 in the People's Choice Podcast Awards. It is one of the Top 40 music podcasts on iTunes and receives over 20,000 downloads of each show. It is hosted by Marc Gunn, known as The Celtfather for his incredible network of promotion for Celtic music. Each hour-long show features a mix of indie Celtic music with a variety of styles from traditional Celtic tunes, Irish drinking songs, Scottish folk songs, bagpipes, music from Ireland, Scotland, Canada, Australia, the United States, and around the world. As a podcast, you can listen to or download at your leisure. It is also syndicated on a number of internet and terrestrial radio stations.

Night Owl Radio
Host: Pasquale Rotella
Frequency: Weekly
Average Show Length: 120 Minutes

Description:
Direct from the Insomniac HQ in Los Angeles, Night Owl Radio is a weekly show presented by the Night Owl aka Pasquale Rotella. With special guest mixes, exclusive info on @insomniacevents, competitions and lots of interaction with You, the Headliners!

The Martin Garrix Show
Host: Martin Garrix
Frequency: Weekly
Average Show Length: 60 Minutes

Description:
A weekly selection of tracks that I love to listen to at home or play out at a party.

Rolling Stone Music Now
Host: Various
Frequency: Weekly
Average Show Length: 45 Minutes

Description:
The writers and editors of Rolling Stone take you inside the biggest stories in music. Featuring interviews with our favorite artists; what's playing in the office; expert insight on the week's biggest music news; and much more.

Helping Friendly Podcast
Host: Various
Frequency: Weekly
Average Show Length: 20 Minutes

Description:
Discussing the music of Phish

Switched on Pop
Hosts: Charlie Harding and Nate Sloan
Frequency: Weekly
Average Show Length: 45 Minutes

Description:
The podcast that explores the making and meaning of popular music hosted by Charlie Harding and Nate Sloan.

The Anjunadeep Edition
Host: Various
Frequency: Weekly
Average Show Length: 60 Minutes

Description:
Plunging into the deepest waters of melodic house, soulful techno and ambient electronica, The Anjunadeep Edition is a weekly 1 hour mix show hosted by the stars of one of dance music's most prolific labels, Anjunadeep.

Marisa Explains It All
Host: Marisa Mendez and Jamal and Tunisia
Frequency: Weekly
Average Show Length: 60 Minutes

Description:
Marisa Mendez and co-hosts Jamal and Tunisia discuss their crazy lives, music, happenings in entertainment and more, sometimes with help from celebrity guests.

Electric For Life
Host: Gareth Emery
Frequency: Weekly
Average Show Length: 60 Minutes

Description:
Electric For Life is the brand new weekly radio show from Gareth Emery.

Lead Singer Syndrome
Host: Shane Told
Frequency: Weekly
Average Show Length: 60 Minutes

Description:
What is it like to be one of the most important members of a band? Shane Told, frontman of the critically-acclaimed rock band Silverstein, brings you candid interviews with all of your favorite singers on this podcast. Is it really all sex, drugs, and rock 'n roll? Find out for yourself on Lead Singer Syndrome.

Beyond Yacht Rock
Hosts: JD Ryznar, David B Lyons, Steve Huey and Hunter Stair
Frequency: Weekly
Average Show Length: 120 Minutes

Description:
From the guys who coined the term Yacht Rock (and brought you the Internet show of the same name) comes a deeper dive into the ocean of arbitrary genres. Every week, J.D. Ryznar, Hunter Stair, "Hollywood" Steve Huey, and David "Koko" Lyons choose a captain to invent a new arbitrary musical genre, and count down the Top Ten songs that define it. And for Yacht Rock fans, every episode also spotlights a bonus Yacht Rock Bone Throw track. Set sail with this crew of music obsessives...there are

treasures to be found! Hosts: JD Ryznar is a Hollywood writer. He knows very little about music, but enjoys imagining elaborate scenarios inspired by popular songs. David B Lyons is a Hollywood Location Manager. He knows a little about music, but feels the need to compartmentalize genres, then rank them. Hollywood Steve Huey is a former staff writer for Allmusic. com, a former talking head for VH1, and currently the only unmarried man on this podcast. Hunter Stair has a mouth that words come out of.

Protocol Radio
Host: Nicky Romero
Frequency: Weekly
Average Show Length: 60 Minutes

Description:
"The main aim is to up my game at every possible turn without compromise." – Nicky Romero "The word wunderkind was pretty much invented for the likes of 24-year-old producer Nicky Romero." – DJMag Now on air every week: Protocol Radio.

Turned Out A Punk
Host: Damian Abraham
Frequency: Weekly
Average Show Length: 60 Minutes

Description:
Damian Abraham can be many things... the singer of a critically acclaimed band, a failed VJ, a host for Vice...a parent, but certainly he is a punk music obsessive. Each week, he sits down and chats with an interesting person from the far reaching worlds of entertainment to find out how their life was changed by the discovery of a novelty genre that supposedly died out in 1978... PUNK.

AOKI's House
Host: Steve Aoki
Frequency: Weekly
Average Show Length: 60 Minutes

Description:
Acclaimed DJ and producer Steve Aoki hosts his own electronic dance music podcast featuring all the latest hot dance tracks.

NEWS & POLITICS

SERIAL

2017 News & Politics Top Pick
SERIAL
Host: Sarah Koenig
Frequency: Daily
Average Show Length:
60 Minutes

Serial is a podcast from the creators of This American Life, hosted by Sarah Koenig. Serial unfolds one story - a true story - over the course of a whole season. The show follows the plot and characters wherever they lead, through many surprising twists and turns. Sarah won't know what happens at the end of the story until she gets there, not long before you get there with her. Each week she'll bring you the latest chapter, so it's important to listen in, starting with Episode 1. New episodes are released on Thursday mornings.

NPR Politics Podcast
Host: Various
Frequency: Daily
Average Show Length: 30 Minutes

Description:
The NPR Politics Podcast is where NPR's political reporters talk to you like they talk to each other. With weekly roundups and quick takes on news of the day, you don't have to keep up with politics to know what's happening. You just have to keep up with us.

Tiny Desk Concerts
Hosts: Jon Favreau, Dan Pfeiffer, Jon Lovett, and Tommy Vietor
Frequency: Daily
Average Show Length: 30 Minutes

Description:
Four former aides to President Obama — Jon Favreau, Dan Pfeiffer, Jon Lovett, and Tommy Vietor — host a Ringer podcast to discuss the political world.

Real Time with Bill Maher

Host: Bill Maher
Frequency: Daily
Average Show Length: 50 Minutes

Description:
Download and watch full episodes of Real Time with Bill Maher including his New Rules and Overtime segments with his guest panelists. New episodes of Real Time with Bill Maher air Fridays at 10, only on HBO.

Breakdown

Host: Bill Rankin
Frequency: Weekly
Average Show Length: 50 Minutes

Description:
Breakdown is just that — the breakdown of the story and the systems. The largest newsroom in the southeast delivers investigations and true crime cases that you cannot find anywhere else.

BBC Global News Podcast

Host: Various
Frequency: Daily
Average Show Length: 50 Minutes

Description:
The day's top stories from BBC News compiled twice daily in the week, once at weekends.

Common Sense with Dan Carlin

Host: Dan Carlin
Frequency: Monthly
Average Show Length: 60 Minutes

Description:
Common Sense with Dan Carlin is an independent look at politics and current events from popular New Media personality Dan Carlin. Carlin's self-described "Martian" viewpoints infuse each episode with a political alien's take on the world around us and the problems it faces. It's a smart, unique (and admittedly U.S.-centric) program that doesn't dumb down the information or analysis for the slowest person in the room. Carlin's

rapid-fire staccato voice has been compared to William Shatner after too many espressos. That, plus his penchant for making everyone in the audience mad at him eventually, makes for a witch's brew of a podcast that is not for everyone. But for those craving a deeper intellectual analysis, a less partisan approach and unpredictable outside-the-box revelations, Common Sense with Dan Carlin is a feast for the mind.

The Ben Shapiro Show
Host: Ben Shapiro
Frequency: Daily
Average Show Length: 60 Minutes

Description:
Podcast by The Daily Wire

CBS This Morning
Hosts: Charlie Rose, Norah O'Donnell and Gayle King
Frequency: Daily
Average Show Length: 60 Minutes

Description:
Start your day with award-winning co-hosts Charlie Rose, Norah O'Donnell and Gayle King in Studio 57 as they bring you the most important headlines, intelligent conversations and world-class original reporting from around the world.

Code Switch
Host: Various
Frequency: Weekly
Average Show Length: 40 Minutes

Description:
Ever find yourself in a conversation about race and identity where you just get...stuck? Code Switch can help. We're all journalists of color, and this isn't just the work we do. It's the lives we lead. Sometimes, we'll make you laugh. Other times, you'll get uncomfortable. But we'll always be unflinchingly honest and empathetic. Come mix it up with us.

Someone Knows Something
Host: David Ridgen
Frequency: Weekly
Average Show Length: 40 Minutes

Description:
SKS is a true-crime podcast, hosted by David Ridgen. Season one investigates the disappearance of five-year-old Adrien McNaughton, who vanished during a fishing trip in 1972. A new season, investigating a new cold case, was released in fall 2016.

1947: The Meet The Press Podcast
Host: Chuck Todd
Frequency: Weekly
Average Show Length: 30 Minutes

Description:
1947 is a new podcast from NBC News, featuring Chuck Todd, Moderator of "Meet the Press." 1947 will feature in-depth conversations with notable figures to go beyond politics. Each episode showcases a single conversation, centered on a guest who has been invited to discuss art, culture, news and of course, politics.

The Axe Files
Host: David Axelrod
Frequency: Daily
Average Show Length: 30 Minutes

Description:
David Axelrod, the founder and director of the University of Chicago Institute of Politics, brings you The Axe Files, a series of revealing interviews with key figures in the political world. Go beyond the soundbites and get to know some of the most interesting players in politics.

Kickass News
Host: Ben Mathis
Frequency: Weekly
Average Show Length: 40 Minutes

Description:
Hosted by Hollywood producer and political media strategist Ben Mathis, KickAss Politics brings together some of the most interesting people from Hollywood to discuss politics, history, technology, world affairs, business,

humor, and more. With nearly 20 years of experience in the movie business and in politics working with Senators, Governors, U.S. Presidents and World Leaders, Ben Mathis brings a unique, fun perspective to politics, culture and current events.

Undisclosed
Host: Various
Frequency: Weekly
Average Show Length: 60 Minutes

Description:
The Undisclosed podcast investigates wrongful convictions, and the U.S. criminal justice system, by taking a closer look at the perpetration of a crime, its investigation, the trial, and ultimate verdict... and finding new evidence that never made it to court.

MSNBC Rachel Maddow
Host: Rachel Maddow
Frequency: Daily
Average Show Length: 40 Minutes

Description:
The Rachel Maddow Show, which airs 9 p.m. ET weeknights on MSNBC, is a smart look at politics, policy, and all the day's top stories. This podcast brings you the audio from each night's show in its entirety.

True Crime Garage
Host: Nic and Captain
Frequency: Weekly
Average Show Length: 60 Minutes

Description:
Each week Nic and the Captain fire up the true crime garage flying ship fueled with beer, great discussion and listener participation. The garage covers a new case each week from headline news to local real life horror stories. Discussions about Serial killers like Ted Bundy, Jeffrey Dahmer and BTK, cold cases like Jonbenet Ramsy, OJ Simpson and the Zodiac, disappearances, missing persons and unsolved mysteries are all on tap along with craft beers from all over the world. If you like to kick back and have a little fun with your true crime than this show is for you and your friends. Remember don't take yourself too seriously because if you do, nobody else will.

The Mark Levin Show Podcast
Host: Mark Levin
Frequency: Daily
Average Show Length: 120 Minutes

Description:
Mark Levin has become one of the hottest properties in Talk radio, his top-rated show on WABC is now syndicated nationally. He is also one of the top new authors in the conservative political arena.

The Sean Hannity Show
Host: Sean Hannity
Frequency: Daily
Average Show Length: 120 Minutes

Description:
Sean Hannity is a multimedia superstar, spending four hours a day every day reaching out to millions of Americans on radio, television and the Internet.

NPR Hourly News Summary
Host: Various
Frequency: Daily
Average Show Length: 5 Minutes

Description:
Five minutes of NPR news, updated hourly.

On Point
Host: Tom Ashbrook
Frequency: Daily
Average Show Length: 50 Minutes

Description:
A live, two-hour morning news-analysis program.

Louder With Crowder
Host: Steven Crowder
Frequency: Weekly
Average Show Length: 120 Minutes

Description:
Steven Crowder brings you news, entertainment and politics with the most

politically incorrect show on the web. Guests, rants, sketches, your calls ... it's whatever.

The Ricochet Podcast
Hosts: James Lileks, Rob Long, and Peter Robinson
Frequency: Weekly
Average Show Length: 60 Minutes

Description:
Weekly episodes of Ricochet's flagship podcast feature our hosts James Lileks, Rob Long, Peter Robinson, and guests discussing the issues of the week. Ricochet offers the best, smartest, most interesting conversations on the web. Both for your eyes and your ears.

The Alex Jones Show
Host: Alex Jones
Frequency: Daily
Average Show Length: 180 Minutes

Description:
Because there's a war on for your mind; veteran broadcaster, filmmaker and media analyst Alex Jones brings you incredible interviews with people on the frontlines of the Infowar and takes an in-depth look at the news between the day's headlines.

Savage Nation
Host: Michael Savage
Frequency: Daily
Average Show Length: 60 Minutes

Description:
Hosted by multimedia icon of the conservative movement, The Savage Nation® delivers a bold perspective on American ideals and culture. Michael Savage has unparalleled determination to unearth the truth about liberalism and national security. His passion for traditional values such as the English language keep listeners tuned-in wherever they are. Savage has repeatedly been named by Talk Stream Live as one of the most influential and most listened-to streaming talk show hosts.

Slate's Political Gabfest

Hosts: Emily Bazelon, John Dickerson and David Plotz
Frequency: Weekly
Average Show Length: 60 Minutes

Description:
Voted "Favorite Political Podcast" by iTunes Listeners. Stephen Colbert says "Everybody should listen to the Slate Political Gabfest." The Gabfest, featuring Slate's Emily Bazelon, John Dickerson, and David Plotz, is the kind of informal and irreverent discussion Washington journalists have after hours over drinks. Part of the Panoply Network.

Vox's The Weeds

Hosts: Ezra Klein, Sarah Kliff and Matthew Yglesias
Frequency: Weekly
Average Show Length: 60 Minutes

Description:
Everyone is always warning you not to get lost in the weeds. But not Vox's Ezra Klein, Sarah Kliff, and Matthew Yglesias. They love the weeds. That's where all the policy is. This is the podcast for people who follow politics because they love thinking about health care, economics, and zoning. It is not a podcast for people who like hearing talk about gaffes.

Democracy Now!

Hosts: Amy Goodman and Juan González
Frequency: Daily
Average Show Length: 60 Minutes

Description:
Democracy Now! is an independent daily TV & radio news program, hosted by award-winning journalists Amy Goodman and Juan González. We provide daily global news headlines, in-depth interviews and investigative reports without any advertisements or government funding. Our programming shines a spotlight on corporate and government abuses of power and lifts up the stories of ordinary people working to make change in extraordinary times.

On The Media
Hosts: Brooke Gladstone and Bob Garfield
Frequency: Daily
Average Show Length: 60 Minutes

Description:
The Peabody Award-winning On the Media podcast is your guide to examining how the media sausage is made. Hosts Brooke Gladstone and Bob Garfield examine threats to free speech and government transparency, cast a skeptical eye on media coverage of the week's big stories and unravel hidden political narratives in everything we read, watch and hear. WNYC Studios is the producer of other leading podcasts including Radiolab, Death, Sex & Money, Freakonomics Radio and many more.

Embedded
Host: Kelly McEvers
Frequency: Daily
Average Show Length: 60 Minutes

Description:
Hosted by Kelly McEvers, Embedded takes a story from the news and goes deep. What does it feel like for a father in El Salvador to lie to his daughter about the bodies he saw in the street that day? What does it feel like for a nurse from rural Indiana to shoot up a powerful prescription opioid? Embedded (EMBD) takes you to where they're happening.

MSNBC Morning Joe
Host: Joe Scarborough
Frequency: Daily
Average Show Length: 40 Minutes

Description:
Wake up every morning with former Florida Congressman Joe Scarborough and the "Morning Joe" team, including MSNBC's Willie Geist and Mika Brzezinski. Subscribe to this audio podcast to get the beginning of each morning's show, ready to go when you are. You'll hear the latest news, political buzz, timely interviews and lots of Joe, Mika and Willie.

The Glenn Beck Program
Host: Glenn Beck
Frequency: Daily
Average Show Length: 40 Minutes

Description:
Listen to The Glenn Beck Radio Program, Monday through Friday.

Perino & Stirewalt: I'll Tell You What
Host: Dana Perino
Frequency: Weekly
Average Show Length: 40 Minutes

Description:
Dana Perino, co-host of The Five on the FOX News Channel and FOX News Digital Politics Editor Chris Stirewalt.

Our National Conversation About Conversations About Race
Hosts: Anna Holmes, Baratunde Thurston, Raquel Cepeda and Tanner Colby
Frequency: Weekly
Average Show Length: 40 Minutes

Description:
Co-discussants Anna Holmes, Baratunde Thurston, Raquel Cepeda and Tanner Colby host a lively multiracial conversation about the ways we can't talk, don't talk, would rather not talk, but intermittently, fitfully, embarrassingly do talk about culture, identity, politics, power, and privilege in our pre-post-yet-still-very-racial America. This show is "About Race."

The Stephen Mansfield Podcast
Host: Stephen Mansfield
Frequency: Weekly
Average Show Length: 15 Minutes

Description:
New York Times bestselling author Stephen Mansfield (The Faith of George W. Bush, The Search for God and Guinness, Lincoln's Battle With God, Mansfield's Book of Manly Men, The Miracle of the Kurds) talks about today's cultural upheavals, trends and ironies, all while providing a fascinating look behind the scenes of his writing and travels.

The Economist Radio
Host: Various
Frequency: Daily
Average Show Length: 30 Minutes

Description:
The Economist was founded in 1843 "to throw white light on the subjects within its range".

The New Yorker: Politics and More
Host: Dorothy Wickenden
Frequency: Daily
Average Show Length: 20 Minutes

Description:
A weekly discussion about politics, hosted by The New Yorker's executive editor, Dorothy Wickenden.

The Ezra Klein Show
Host: Ezra Klein
Frequency: Weekly
Average Show Length: 90 Minutes

Description:
Ezra Klein gives you a chance to get inside the heads of the newsmakers and power players in politics and media. These are extended conversations with policymakers, writers, technologists, and business leaders about what they believe in and why. Look elsewhere for posturing confrontation and quick reactions to the day's news. Subscribe for the anti-soundbite.

RELIGION & SPIRITUALITY

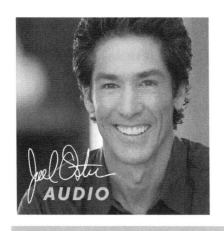

2017 Religion & Spirituality Top Pick

JOEL OLSTEEN

Host: Joel Olsteen
Frequency: Weekly
Average Show Length: 30 Minutes

Welcome to the weekly audio Podcast from Joel Osteen. Joel and Victoria Osteen are pastors of Lakewood Church in Houston, Texas, a vibrant and diverse church that Forbes calls the largest and fastest - growing congregation in America.

Harry Potter and the Sacred Text
Hosts: Vanessa Zoltan and Casper ter Kuile
Frequency: Weekly
Average Show Length: 25 Minutes

Description:
What if we read the books we love as if they were sacred texts? What would we learn? How might they change us? Harry Potter and the Sacred Text is a podcast reading Harry Potter, the best-selling series of all time, as if it was a sacred text. Just as Christians read the Bible, Jews the Torah and Muslims read the Quran, we will embark on a 199-episode journey (one chapter an episode, to be released weekly) to glean what wisdom and meaning J.K. Rowling's beloved novels have for us today. We will read Harry Potter, not just as novels, but as instructive and inspirational texts that will teach us about our own lives.

Pastor Rick's Daily Hope
Host: Rick Warren
Frequency: Weekly
Average Show Length: 25 Minutes

Description:
Learn, Love, and LIVE the Word! Join Rick Warren Monday-Friday as he presents practical and applicable teaching from God's Word that will give you daily hope. Apply biblical wisdom to your marriage, children, spiritual growth, hurts, habits, and purpose on this earth. Listen every day for your daily hope.

Elevation Church Podcast
Host: Pastor Steven Furtick
Frequency: Weekly
Average Show Length: 45 Minutes

Description:
Welcome to the weekly podcast of Elevation Church led by Pastor Steven Furtick.

Gospel In Life
Host: Timothy Keller
Frequency: Monthly
Average Show Length: 45 Minutes

Description:
Classic sermons by Tim Keller, Pastor of Redeemer Presbyterian Church in New York City and NY Times best-selling author of "The Reason for God: Belief in an Age of Skepticism.

Tara Brach
Host: Tara Brach
Frequency: Daily
Average Show Length: 30 Minutes

Description:
Tara Brach is a leading western teacher of Buddhist (mindfulness) meditation, emotional healing and spiritual awakening. She is author of Radical Acceptance (2003), and True Refuge (2013). Senior teacher at the Insight Meditation Community of Washington D.C. (IMCW), Tara shares a weekly talk on Buddhist teachings and practices.

The Village Church Sermons
Host: Matt Chandler
Frequency: Weekly
Average Show Length: 50 Minutes

Description:
The Village Church exists to bring glory to God by making disciples through gospel-centered worship, gospel-centered community, gospel-centered service and gospel-centered multiplication.

Enjoying Everyday Life
Host: Joyce Meyer
Frequency: Weekly
Average Show Length: 30 Minutes

Description:
Enjoying Everyday Life is a daily TV and radio broadcast provided by Joyce Meyer Ministries.

The Liturgists Podcast
Hosts: Michael Gungor, Mike McHargue and Lissa Paino
Frequency: Weekly
Average Show Length: 60 Minutes

Description:
Michael Gungor, Science Mike, Lissa Paino, and an ever revolving cast of creators take on topics through the perspectives of science, art, and faith.

Your Move
Host: Andy Stanley
Frequency: Weekly
Average Show Length: 30 Minutes

Description:
Welcome to the Your Move with Andy Stanley podcast. In this weekly 30-minute message from Andy, you will discover how to make better decisions and live with fewer regrets. So check out our website at www.yourmove.is for additional ways to watch, listen, and connect.

Andy Stanley Leadership Podcast
Host: Andy Stanley
Frequency: Monthly
Average Show Length: 30 Minutes

Description:
Welcome to the Andy Stanley Leadership Podcast, a conversation designed to help leaders go further, faster. Andy Stanley is a pastor, communicator, author, and the founder of North Point Ministries in Alpharetta, Georgia.

Let My People Think
Host: Bob Zacharias
Frequency: Weekly
Average Show Length: 30 Minutes

Description:
Let My People Think with Ravi Zacharias is a 30-minute radio program from Ravi Zacharias International Ministries that powerfully mixes biblical teaching and Christian apologetics. The program from RZIM seeks to explore issues such as life's meaning, the credibility of the Christian message and the Bible, the weakness of modern intellectual movements, and the uniqueness of Jesus Christ.

The RobCast
Host: Rob Bell
Frequency: Weekly
Average Show Length: 60 Minutes

Description:
The RobCast is a weekly podcast by Rob Bell

John Piper Sermons
Host: John Piper
Frequency: Weekly
Average Show Length: 60 Minutes

Description:
John Piper is founder and teacher of desiringGod.org; he is author of more than 50 books and travels regularly to preach and teach. New messages are posted to this podcast as they become available. We want people everywhere to understand and embrace the truth that God is most glorified in us, when we are most satisfied in him.

Bethel
Host: Bill Johnson
Frequency: Weekly
Average Show Length: 60 Minutes

Description:
Bethel Church is a community of believers led by pastor Bill Johnson in Redding, California. We are passionate about God and people. Our mission is revival: the personal, regional, and global expansion of God's Kingdom through his manifest presence.

Read Scripture
Host: Francis Chan
Frequency: Weekly
Average Show Length: 30 Minutes

Description:
Read Scripture with Francis Chan, best-selling author of Crazy Love, Forgotten God, Erasing Hell, Multiply, and You and Me Forever. Currently, he is planting churches in the San Francisco area.

Craig Groeschel Leadership Podcast
Host: Craig Groeschel
Frequency: Monthly
Average Show Length: 20 Minutes

Description:
Welcome to the Craig Groeschel Leadership Podcast, a conversation designed to help you make the most of your potential as you work to become the leader God created you to be. Craig Groeschel is a speaker, author, and the Senior Pastor of Life.Church.

Mindful Living Spiritual Awakening
Host: Marijo Puleo, PHD
Frequency: Weekly
Average Show Length: 50 Minutes

Description:
For people interested in mindfulness and meditation and experiencing aspects of spiritual awakening. Learn practical ways to meditate; explore your intuitive talents; helpful life skills; and science that supports these experiences.

The Potter's Touch
Host: Bishop T.D. Jakes
Frequency: Weekly
Average Show Length: 30 Minutes

Description:
The Potter's Touch, a weekly program, with Bishop T.D. Jakes, tackles today's topics and confronts the hidden issues and invisible scars that go untreated. This broadcast carries healing and restoration into homes of hurting people, unearthing taboo topics and offering practical and spiritual solutions to life's toughest questions.

Culture Matters
Host: Matt Chandler
Frequency: Weekly
Average Show Length: 60 Minutes

Description:
Matters of culture should matter to us—because they matter to God. Hosted by Matt Chandler and Josh Patterson, the Culture Matters podcast explores the intersection of faith and culture. Looking at everything from politics, art and entertainment to issues such as racial reconciliation and the sanctity of human life, we discuss what it looks like to live faithfully on mission—in the world but not of the world.

Renewing Your Mind
Host: R.C. Sproul
Frequency: Daily
Average Show Length: 25 Minutes

Description:
Since 1994, Renewing Your Mind with Dr. R.C. Sproul has provided accessible, in-depth Bible teaching to millions around the world. As the principal outreach of Ligonier Ministries, this radio broadcast has instructed listeners in the life-changing truths of historic Christianity and has kept the church community informed about pertinent issues facing believers today.

The Happy Hour
Host: Jamie Ivey
Frequency: Weekly
Average Show Length: 60 Minutes

Description:
The Happy Hour Podcast is hosted by Jamie Ivey, and each week she brings a guest to the show. During the happy hour they will discuss anything and everything just as if you were around the table with your own girlfriends. Jamie loves to connect with women and encourage them as they journey through life. These conversations will make you laugh and cry all in one. The Happy Hour will be something you look forward to each week. You will be encouraged as you listen to other women talk about the simplest things in life to the grandest. Grab a cup of coffee and enjoy the conversation!

Truth For Life
Host: Alistair Begg
Frequency: Weekly
Average Show Length: 30 Minutes

Description:
Truth For Life is the Bible-teaching ministry of Alistair Begg. The ministry's mission is to teach the Bible with clarity and relevance so that unbelievers will be converted, believers will be established and local churches will be strengthened. Join us each weekday and on the weekend as Alistair helps us apply the Scripture to our daily lives.

Catholic Stuff You Should Know
Host: Various
Frequency: Weekly
Average Show Length: 50 Minutes

Description:
A lighthearted exploration of various prominent and obscure Catholic topics.

Fear Based Life
Host: Melissa Stephens
Frequency: Weekly
Average Show Length: 90 Minutes

Description:
After a spiritual breakdown Melissa Stephens explores her fears, phobias, beliefs and seeks solace from anyone.

Fresh Life Church
Host: Pastor Levi Lusko
Frequency: Weekly
Average Show Length: 60 Minutes

Description:
This is the podcast of the teachings of Fresh Life Church in Kalispell Montana with Pastor Levi Lusko. they are simply messages from the Word of God, real. relevant. raw.

Ask Pastor John
Host: Pastor John Piper
Frequency: Weekly
Average Show Length: 15 Minutes

Description:
Daily audio clips of John Piper answering tough theological and pastoral questions.

The Urban Alternative
Host: Dr. Tory Evans
Frequency: Weekly
Average Show Length: 30 Minutes

Description:
The Urban Alternative is the national ministry of Dr. Tony Evans and is dedicated to restoring hope and transforming lives through the proclamation and application of the Word of God.

UMD Newman Catholic Campus Ministry
Host: Father Mike Schmitz
Frequency: Weekly
Average Show Length: 30 Minutes

Description:
Homilies preached by Fr. Michael Schmitz, Chaplain for the University of Minnesota-Duluth Catholic Campus Ministry.

James MacDonald: Walk in the Word
Host: James MacDonald
Frequency: Daily
Average Show Length: 30 Minutes

Description:
Welcome to the podcast and Bible-teaching ministry of Dr. James MacDonald, Pastor of Harvest Bible Chapel in the suburbs of Chicago and teacher of the daily Walk in the Word broadcast. James MacDonald's ministries emphasize the precise exposition and life application of God's Word. Whether from behind the pulpit or through audio, video, web, printed resources, and events, his personal and practical teaching leads people to the transforming power of God's Word.

The BadChristian Podcast
Hosts: Various
Frequency: Weekly
Average Show Length: 90 Minutes

Description:
Matt, Toby and Joey discuss funny, controversial, and personal stuff with guests from the music business, leaders in the Christian world, and interesting folks from well outside of the Christian world. In other words... REAL TALK. I Bad Christian The language and topics used in this podcast are for mature listeners. Listen at your own discretion.

North Point Community Church
Hosts: Various
Frequency: Weekly
Average Show Length: 45 Minutes

Description:
Welcome to the weekly audio podcast for North Point Community
Church in Alpharetta, GA where our mission is to lead people into a
growing relationship with Jesus Christ. Our desire is that this podcast will
encourage you in your relationship with God.

The Word on Fire Show
Host: Bishop Robert Barron
Frequency: Weekly
Average Show Length: 30 Minutes

Description:
Join Bishop Robert Barron for a weekly podcast on faith and culture.

The Glorious in the Mundane
Host: Christy Nockels
Frequency: Weekly
Average Show Length: 30 Minutes

Description:
The "Glorious in the Mundane" podcast is hosted by Christian Artist and
Worship Leader Christy Nockels. Offering conversations and interviews
with some of your favorite artists, speakers and authors, the podcast is
designed to inspire you right where you are today doing whatever it is
you're doing.

The One You Feed
Host: Eric Zimmer
Frequency: Weekly
Average Show Length: 45 Minutes

Description:
Conversations about Creating a Life Worth Living- Named Best of 2014
by iTunes. Open minded discussions of habits, meditation, wisdom,
depression, anxiety, happiness, psychology, philosophy, and motivation.

Pass The Mic
Host: Various
Frequency: Weekly
Average Show Length: 50 Minutes

Description:
Pass The Mic is the premier podcast of the Reformed African American Network. Tune in every week for engaging discussions and high profile interviews addressing the core concerns of African Americans biblically.

SCIENCE & MEDICINE

2017 Science & Medicine Top Pick

STAR TALK

Host: Neil deGrasse Tyson

Frequency: Weekly

Average Show Length: 60 Minutes

Science meets comedy and pop culture on StarTalk Radio! Astrophysicist and Hayden Planetarium director Neil deGrasse Tyson, his comic co-hosts, guest celebrities and scientists discuss astronomy, physics, and everything else about life in the universe. But wait... there's more! Our new show, StarTalk All-Stars, features a revolving slate of all-star scientists and science educators including Bill Nye the Science Guy, backed up by your favorite comic co-hosts.

Hidden Brain

Host: Shankar Vedantam

Frequency: Weekly

Average Show Length: 30 Minutes

Description:

The Hidden Brain helps curious people understand the world – and themselves. Using science and storytelling, Hidden Brain's host Shankar Vedantam reveals the unconscious patterns that drive human behavior, the biases that shape our choices, and the triggers that direct the course of our relationships.

Radiolab
Hosts: Jad Abumrad and Robert Krulwich
Frequency: Weekly
Average Show Length: 60 Minutes

Description:
A two-time Peabody Award-winner, Radiolab is an investigation told through sounds and stories, and centered around one big idea. In the Radiolab world, information sounds like music and science and culture collide. Hosted by Jad Abumrad and Robert Krulwich, the show is designed for listeners who demand skepticism, but appreciate wonder. WNYC Studios is the producer of other leading podcasts including Freakonomics Radio, Death, Sex & Money, On the Media and many more.

Invisibilia
Hosts: Lulu Miller, Hanna Rosin and Alix Spiegel
Frequency: Weekly
Average Show Length: 60 Minutes

Description:
Invisibilia (Latin for invisible things) is about the invisible forces that control human behavior – ideas, beliefs, assumptions and emotions. Co-hosted by Lulu Miller, Hanna Rosin and Alix Spiegel, Invisibilia interweaves narrative storytelling with scientific research that will ultimately make you see your own life differently.

Sword and Scale
Host: Mike Boudet
Frequency: Weekly
Average Show Length: 60 Minutes

Description:
The Sword and Scale true-crime podcast is an immersive audio experience covering the underworld of criminal activity and the demented minds that perform the most despicable and unthinkable actions, proving that the worst monsters are very real. We cover true-crime stories, high-profile trials, unsolved murders and missing persons cases.

Science VS

Host: Wendy Zukerman
Frequency: Weekly
Average Show Length: 30 Minutes

Description:
There are a lot of fads, blogs and strong opinions, but then there's SCIENCE. Science Vs is the new show from Gimlet Media that finds out what's fact, what's not, and what's somewhere in between. We do the hard work of sifting through all the science so you don't have to. This season we'll be tackling organic food, fracking, gun control, the G spot, and more.

Science Friday

Host: Ira Flatow
Frequency: Weekly
Average Show Length: 45 Minutes

Description:
Covering everything about science and technology -- from the outer reaches of space to the tiniest microbes in our bodies -- Science Friday is your source for entertaining and educational stories and activities. Each week, host Ira Flatow interviews scientists and inventors like Sylvia Earle, Elon Musk, Neil deGrasse Tyson, and more.

How To Do Everything

Host: Mike Danforth and Ian Chillag
Frequency: Weekly
Average Show Length: 20 Minutes

Description:
We're half advice show, half survival guide. We answer all your questions, from how to find a date, to how to find water in the desert.

TEDTalks Science and Medicine
Host: Various
Frequency: Weekly
Average Show Length: 15 Minutes

Description:
Some of the world's greatest scientists, doctors and medical researchers share their discoveries and visions onstage at the TED conference, TEDx events and partner events around the world. You can also download these and many other videos free on TED.com, with an interactive English transcript and subtitles in up to 80 languages. TED is a nonprofit devoted to Ideas Worth Spreading.

Stuff To Blow Your Mind
Hosts: Christian Sager, Robert Lamb and Joe McCormick
Frequency: Weekly
Average Show Length: 90 Minutes

Description:
Deep in the back of your mind, you've always had the feeling that there's something strange about reality. There is. Join Robert, Joe and Christian as they examine neurological quandaries, cosmic mysteries, evolutionary marvels and our transhuman future on Stuff To Blow Your Mind, a podcast from HowStuffWorks.com.

BrainStuff
Host: Various
Frequency: Weekly
Average Show Length: 5 Minutes

Description:
Whether the topic is popcorn or particle physics, you can count on BrainStuff to explore -- and explain -- the everyday science in the world around us.

Weekly Infusion
Hosts: Dr. Drew Pinsky, and Dr. Bruce Heischober
Frequency: Weekly
Average Show Length: 45 Minutes

Description:
Weekly Infusion, hosted by board certified internists, Dr. Drew Pinsky, and Dr. Bruce Heischober, focuses on all things medicine and science. Each

week, the doctors tackle a different subject with sensitivity and humor. Expert guests are on hand to help demystify and simplify topics that range from everyday health issues, to the latest medical breakthroughs and treatments, to incredible stories of the ER.

Mysterious Universe
Host: Benjamin Grundy
Frequency: Weekly
Average Show Length: 90 Minutes

Description:
Mysterious Universe brings you the latest news and podcasts covering the strange, extraordinary, weird, wonderful and everything in between.

The Psychology Podcast
Host: Dr. Scott Barry Kaufman
Frequency: Weekly
Average Show Length: 35 Minutes

Description:
Welcome to The Psychology Podcast with Dr. Scott Barry Kaufman, where we give you insights into the mind, brain, behavior and creativity. Each episode we'll feature a guest who will stimulate your mind, and give you a greater understanding of yourself, others, and the world we live in. Hopefully, we'll also provide a glimpse into human possibility!

Flash Forward
Host: Rose Eveleth
Frequency: Weekly
Average Show Length: 40 Minutes

Description:
A show about possible and not so possible futures. From space pirates to conscious robots to the end of antibiotics. Hosted by Rose Eveleth.

60 Second Science
Host: Steve Mirsky
Frequency: Daily
Average Show Length: 2 Minutes

Description:
Leading science journalists provide a daily minute commentary on some of the most interesting developments in the world of science. For a full-length, weekly podcast you can subscribe to Science Talk: The Podcast of Scientific American.

The Infinite Monkey Cage
Hosts: Brian Cox and Robin Ince
Frequency: Weekly
Average Show Length: 45 Minutes

Description:
Witty, irreverent look at the world through scientists' eyes. With Brian Cox and Robin Ince.

The Paranormal Podcast
Host: Jim Harold
Frequency: Weekly
Average Show Length: 60 Minutes

Description:
America's Top Paranormal Podcaster interviews the best known names in the paranormal about UFOs, Ghosts, Bigfoot, and everything paranormal! Guests have included Amy Bruni, Chip Coffey, George Noory and the biggest names in paranormal studies. This feed reflects the last 90 days of content, The Paranormal Podcast has been in production since 2005 with over 400 episodes. Hosted by Jim Harold.

Data Skeptic
Host: Kyle Polich
Frequency: Weekly
Average Show Length: 30 Minutes

Description:
The Data Skeptic Podcast features interviews and discussion of topics related to data science, statistics, machine learning, artificial intelligence and the like, all from the perspective of applying critical thinking and the scientific method to evaluate the veracity of claims and efficacy of

approaches.

You Are Not So Smart
Host: David McRaney
Frequency: Weekly
Average Show Length: 60 Minutes

Description:
You Are Not So Smart is a celebration of self delusion that explores topics related to cognitive biases, heuristics, and logical fallacies. David McRaney interviews scientists about their research into how the mind works, and then he eats a cookie.

Nature Podcast
Host: Kerri Smith
Frequency: Weekly
Average Show Length: 30 Minutes

Description:
The Nature Podcast brings you the best stories from the world of science each week. We cover everything from astronomy to neuroscience, highlighting the most exciting research from each issue of Nature journal. We meet the scientists behind the results and provide in-depth analysis from Nature's journalists and editors.

Real Ghost Stories Online
Hosts: Tony Brueski and Jenny Brueski
Frequency: Weekly
Average Show Length: 60 Minutes

Description:
A daily paranormal podcast filled with real ghost stories of horror, told by real people. Stories that encompass all areas of the paranormal, supernatural, demonic, ghost investigations, haunted houses, possessions, shadow people, unexplained and more.

EMCrit Podcast
Host: Various
Frequency: Weekly
Average Show Length: 20 Minutes

Description:
Help me fill in the blanks of the practice of ED Critical Care. In this podcast, we discuss all things related to the crashing, critically ill patient in the Emergency Department.

Inquiring Minds
Host: Indre Viskontas
Frequency: Weekly
Average Show Length: 60 Minutes

Description:
Each week Inquiring Minds brings you a new, in-depth exploration of the place where science, politics, and society collide. We're committed to the idea that making an effort to understand the world around you though science and critical thinking can benefit everyone—and lead to better decisions. We endeavor to find out what's true, what's left to discover, and why it all matters with weekly coverage of the latest headlines and probing discussions with leading scientists and thinkers.

Warm Regards
Host: Eric Holthaus
Frequency: Weekly
Average Show Length: 30 Minutes

Description:
Warm Regards is a podcast about the warming planet. The show is hosted by meteorologist Eric Holthaus. Co-hosts are Jacquelyn Gill, a paleoecologist at the University of Maine, and Andy Revkin, a veteran journalist at the New York Times.

Science Magazine Podcast
Host: Various
Frequency: Weekly
Average Show Length: 20 Minutes

Description:
Weekly podcasts from Science Magazine, the world's leading journal of original scientific research, global news, and commentary.

The Story Collider
Host: Farah Ahmad
Frequency: Weekly
Average Show Length: 15 Minutes

Description:
Our lives revolve around science. From passing high school chemistry to surviving open-heart surgery, from reading a book on mountain lions to seeing the aftermath of an oil spill, from spinning a top to looking at pictures of distant galaxies, science affects us and shapes us. At The Story Collider, we want to know people's stories about science. From our monthly live shows to our Pictures of Science project, we bring together scientists, comedians, librarians, and other disreputable types to tell true, personal stories of times when, for good or ill, science happened.

This Week I Learned
Host: Lauren Hansen
Frequency: Weekly
Average Show Length: 10 Minutes

Description:
This weekly podcast series is your audio guide to the most fascinating and fun revelations, reports, and studies on the internet. Quick, concise, and infectiously entertaining, This Week I Learned promises to make learning fun again. New episodes: every Friday.

Emergency Medicine Cases
Host: Dr. Anton Helman
Frequency: Weekly
Average Show Length: 60 Minutes

Description:
In-depth round table discussions with two or more of Canada's brightest minds in Emergency Medicine on practical practice changing EM topics since 2010.

Astronomy Cast
Hosts: Fraser Cain and Dr. Pamela L. Gay
Frequency: Weekly
Average Show Length: 30 Minutes

Description:
Astronomy Cast brings you a weekly fact-based journey through the cosmos.

Discovery
Host: Various
Frequency: Weekly
Average Show Length: 30 Minutes

Description:
Explorations in the world of science.

Minute Physics
Host: Henry Reich
Frequency: Weekly
Average Show Length: 1 Minute

Description
Cool physics and other sweet science - all in a minute!

Science Talk
Host: Steve Mirsky
Frequency: Weekly
Average Show Length: 30 Minutes

Description:
Science Talk is a weekly science audio show covering the latest in the world of science and technology. Join Steve Mirsky each week as he explores cutting-edge breakthroughs and controversial issues with leading scientists and journalists. He is also an articles editor and columnist at Scientific American magazine.

The Guardian's Science Weekly
Hosts: Ian Sample, Hannah Devlin and Nicola Davis
Frequency: Weekly
Average Show Length: 30 Minutes

Description:
The award winning Science Weekly is the best place to learn about the big discoveries and debates in biology, chemistry, physics, and sometimes even maths. From the Guardian science desk Ian Sample, Hannah Devlin & Nicola Davis meet the great thinkers and doers in science and technology. Science has never sounded so good!

Only Human
Host: Mary Harris
Frequency: Weekly
Average Show Length: 30 Minutes

Description:
Only Human is a podcast about making the most of our health, whether we're training for a marathon, overcoming an illness, or trying not to go broke paying for healthcare. Hosted by Mary Harris, Only Human is a show where we're not afraid to have uncomfortable conversations, and experiment with possible solutions. Only Human. Because everybody has a story. WNYC Studios is the producer of leading podcasts including Radiolab, Death, Sex & Money, Freakonomics Radio, On the Media and many others.

The Skeptics' Guide to the Universe
Host: Dr. Steven Novella
Frequency: Weekly
Average Show Length: 90 Minutes

Description:
The Skeptics' Guide to the Universe is a weekly science podcast discussing the latest science news, critical thinking, bad science, conspiracies and controversies. -The Skeptics' Guide to the Universe: Your escape to reality.

Physician Assistant Boards Podcast
Host: Various
Frequency: Weekly
Average Show Length: 30 Minutes

Description:
Physicianassistantboards.com is dedicated to providing free medical content to help you pass all of your exams, with one final goal in mind: success on your boards.

Planetary Radio
Host: Various
Frequency: Weekly
Average Show Length: 46 Minutes

Description:
Each week, Planetary Radio visits with a scientist, engineer, project manager, advocate or writer who can provide a unique perspective on the quest for knowledge about astronomy, our solar system and beyond. We also showcase regular features that raise your space IQ while they put a smile on your face. In addition, host Mat Kaplan is joined every week by Planetary Society colleagues Bill Nye the Science Guy, Bruce Betts, and Emily Lakdawalla to discuss the latest news about NASA and the Planetary Society.

All In The Mind
Hosts: Rick Rohan and Duane Beeman
Frequency: Weekly
Average Show Length: 30 Minutes

Description:
All In The Mind is Radio National's weekly foray into the mental universe, the mind, brain and behaviour - everything from addiction to artificial intelligence.

Skeptoid
Host: Brian Dunning
Frequency: Weekly
Average Show Length: 15 Minutes

Description:
Since 2006, the weekly Skeptoid podcast has been taking on all the most popular myths and revealing the true science, true history, and true lessons we can learn from each.

Sasquatch Chronicles
Host: Wes Germer
Frequency: Weekly
Average Show Length: 120 Minutes

Description:
Join us as we discuss recent Sasquatch sightings, encounters and talk to Bigfoot eye witnesses. People are seeing something in the woods and there are too many reports for this too be ignored. Listen as we talk to researchers, witnesses and investigators to unravel the mystery of Bigfoot. Every week we will also bring you the latest Bigfoot news and information.

SOCIETY & CULTURE

2017 Society & Culture
Top Pick
FRESH AIR
Host: Ira Glass
Frequency: Weekly
Average Show Length:
60 Minutes

This American Life is a weekly public radio show, heard by 2.2 million people on more than 500 stations. Another 1.5 million people download the weekly podcast. It is hosted by Ira Glass, produced in collaboration with Chicago Public Media, delivered to stations by PRX The Public Radio Exchange, and has won all of the major broadcasting awards.

Stuff You Should Know
Hosts: Josh Clark and Chuck Bryant
Frequency: Weekly
Average Show Length: 45 Minutes

Description:
How do landfills work? How do mosquitos work? Join Josh and Chuck as they explore the Stuff You Should Know about everything from genes to the Galapagos in this podcast from HowStuffWorks.com.

Freakonomics Radio
Host: Stephen J. Dubner
Frequency: Weekly
Average Show Length: 45 Minutes

Description:
Have fun discovering the hidden side of everything with host Stephen J. Dubner, co-author of the best-selling "Freakonomics" books. Each week, hear surprising conversations that explore the riddles of everyday life and the weird wrinkles of human nature—from cheating and crime to parenting and sports.

Dan Carlin's Hardcore History

Host: Dan Carlin
Frequency: Quarterly
Average Show Length: 4 Hours

Description:
In "Hardcore History" journalist and broadcaster Dan Carlin takes his "Martian", unorthodox way of thinking and applies it to the past. Was Alexander the Great as bad a person as Adolf Hitler? What would Apaches with modern weapons be like? Will our modern civilization ever fall like civilizations from past eras? This isn't academic history (and Carlin isn't a historian) but the podcast's unique blend of high drama, masterful narration and Twilight Zone-style twists has entertained millions of listeners.

Stuff You Missed in History Class

Hosts: Holly Fray and Tracy Wilson
Frequency: Weekly
Average Show Length: 45 Minutes

Description:
Join Holly and Tracy as they bring you the greatest and strangest Stuff You Missed In History Class in this podcast by HowStuffWorks.com.

Women of the Hour

Host: Lena Dunham
Frequency: Weekly
Average Show Length: 60 Minutes

Description:
Lena Dunham hosts this podcast miniseries about friendship, love, work, bodies and more.

Tell Me Something I Don't Know

Host: Stephen J. Dubner
Frequency: Weekly
Average Show Length: 60 Minutes

Description:
Join host Stephen J. Dubner of "Freakonomics Radio" and three celebrity panelists as they invite contestants on stage to tell us something we don't know. It could be a fascinating fact, a historical wrinkle, a new line of research — anything, really, long as it's interesting, useful and true (or at least true-ish). There's a real-time human fact-checker on hand to filter out

the bull. The panel — an eclectic mix of comedians, brainiacs, and other high achievers — will poke and prod the contestants and ultimately choose a winner. Like the "Freakonomics" podcast and books, "Tell Me Something I Don't Know" is still journalism, still factual — but disguised in the most entertaining, unexpected and occasionally ridiculous conversation you're likely to hear. Produced in partnership with The New York Times.

Revisionist History
Host: Malcolm Gladwell
Frequency: Weekly
Average Show Length: 30 Minutes

Description:
Join host Stephen J. Dubner of "Freakonomics Radio" and three celebrity panelists as they invite contestants on stage to tell us something we don't know. It could be a fascinating fact, a historical wrinkle, a new line of research — anything, really, long as it's interesting, useful and true (or at least true-ish). There's a real-time human fact-checker on hand to filter out the bull.

Lore
Host: Aaron Mahnke
Frequency: Weekly
Average Show Length: 30 Minutes

Description:
Lore is a bi-weekly podcast (and upcoming TV show) about the dark historical tales that fuel our modern superstitions. Each episode explores the world of mysterious creatures, tragic events, and unusual places. Because sometimes the truth is more frightening than fiction.

Criminal
Host: Phoebe Judge
Frequency: Weekly
Average Show Length: 30 Minutes

Description:
Criminal is a podcast about crime. Not so much the "if it bleeds, it leads," kind of crime. Something a little more complex. Stories of people who've done wrong, been wronged, and/or gotten caught somewhere in the middle.

Remarkable Lives. Tragic Deaths.
Hosts: Carter Roy and Vanessa Richardson
Frequency: Weekly
Average Show Length: 45 Minutes

Description:
We examine the lives and deaths of prominent people who changed history and influenced pop culture. We tell you their story, their achievements, their struggles, their secrets and take you on dramatic journey through the life and ultimate tragic death of those who have had an impact on society. With the help of voice actors, we attempt to honor these individuals by bringing their stories to life. New episodes are released every Wednesday.

The New Yorker Radio Hour
Host: David Remnick
Frequency: Weekly
Average Show Length: 55 Minutes

Description:
David Remnick is joined by The New Yorker's award-winning writers, editors, and artists to present a weekly mix of profiles, storytelling, and insightful conversations about the issues that matter — plus an occasional blast of comic genius from the magazine's legendary Shouts and Murmurs page. The New Yorker has set a standard in journalism for generations, and The New Yorker Radio Hour gives it a voice on public radio for the first time. Produced by The New Yorker and WNYC Studios. WNYC studios is the producer of leading podcasts including Radiolab, Freakonomics Radio, Note To Self, Here's The Thing With Alec Baldwin, and more.

The History of Rome
Host: Mike Duncan
Frequency: Weekly
Average Show Length: 30 Minutes

Description:
A weekly podcast tracing the history of the Roman Empire, beginning with Aeneas's arrival in Italy and ending with the exile of Romulus Augustulus, last Emperor of the Western Roman Empire. Now complete!

The Art of Manliness
Host: Brett McKay
Frequency: Weekly
Average Show Length: 45 Minutes

Description:
The Art of Manliness podcast features discussions on topics and issues important or of interest to men. The goal of the podcast is to help men become better men.

Something You Should Know
Host: Mike Carruthers
Frequency: Weekly
Average Show Length: 30 Minutes

Description:
A single fact, a small piece of intel or a bit of sage advice can transform your life for the better. Something You Should Know is dedicated to delivering the most fascinating information from top experts around the world in a fun and entertaining podcast. Here you'll discover ways to save time and money, be more efficient, grow your business, be a better parent and simply navigate the world better. Long-time radio host, Mike Carruthers has crafted an all-new podcast for people who crave information they can actually use in their lives.

The Way I Heard It
Host: Mike Rowe
Frequency: Weekly
Average Show Length: 10 Minutes

Description:
All good stories have a twist, and all great storytellers are just a little twisted. Join Mike Rowe for a different take on the people and events that you thought you knew -- from pop-culture to politics from Hollywood to History... The Way I Heard It with Mike Rowe -- short mysteries for the curious mind with a short attention span.

On Being with Krista Tippett
Host: Krista Tippett
Frequency: Weekly
Average Show Length: 60 Minutes

Description:
On Being takes up the big questions of meaning with scientists and theologians, artists and teachers — some you know and others you'll love to meet. Each week a new discovery about the immensity of our lives — updated every Thursday. Hosted by Krista Tippett.

Casefile
Host: Various
Frequency: Weekly
Average Show Length: 60 Minutes

Description:
Fact is scarier than fiction. Casefile, a new true crime podcast. Each episode explores a new case. We cover the shocking, the terrifying, the strange, and the unsolved.

Heavyweight
Host: Jonathan Goldstein
Frequency: Weekly
Average Show Length: 30 Minutes

Description:
Maybe you've laid awake imagining how it could have been, how it might yet be, but the moment to act was never right. Well, the moment is here and the podcast making it happen is Heavyweight. Join Jonathan Goldstein for road trips, thorny reunions, and difficult conversations as he backpedals his way into the past like a therapist with a time machine. From Gimlet Media.

BackStory
Hosts: Ed Ayers, Peter Onuf and Brian Balogh
Frequency: Weekly
Average Show Length: 30 Minutes

Description:
BackStory with the American History Guys is a nationally syndicated, hour-long, weekly public radio show hosted by renowned U.S. historians Ed Ayers, Peter Onuf, and Brian Balogh. We're based in Charlottesville,

Virginia at the Virginia Foundation for the Humanities. Each week we take a topic that people are talking about and explore its roots in American history. Through stories, interviews, and conversation with our listeners, we turn the things Americans take for granted inside out. And we have a lot of fun.

Modern Love
Host: Meghna Chakrabarti
Frequency: Weekly
Average Show Length: 20 Minutes

Description:
Stories of love, loss and redemption

Death, Sex & Money
Host: Anna Sale
Frequency: Weekly
Average Show Length: 45 Minutes

Description:
Death, Sex & Money is a podcast about the big questions and hard choices that are often left out of polite conversation. Host Anna Sale talks to celebrities you've heard of—and to regular people you haven't—about the Big Stuff: relationships, money, family, work and making it all count while we're here. WNYC Studios is the producer of other leading podcasts including Freakonomics Radio, Note to Self, Here's the Thing with Alec Baldwin and many others.

Terrible, Thanks For Asking
Host: Nora McInerny Purmort
Frequency: Weekly
Average Show Length: 45 Minutes

Description:
You know how every day someone asks "how are you?" And even if you're totally dying inside, you just say "fine," so everyone can go about their day? This show is the opposite of that. Hosted by author and notable widow (her words) Nora McInerny Purmort, this is a funny/sad/uncomfortable podcast about talking honestly about our pain, our awkwardness, and our humanness, which is not an actual word.

Presidents Are People Too!
Host: Alexis Coe
Frequency: Weekly
Average Show Length: 25 Minutes

Description:
The Audible Originals series Presidents Are People Too! recasts each of the American Presidents as real-life people, complete with flaws, quirks, triumphs, scandals and bodily ailments. Hosts Elliott Kalan, former Daily Show head writer, and American historian and author Alexis Coe talk to experts, comedians, journalists, actors and re-enactors to better understand the men memorialized on the Washington Mall and those all but forgotten.

Unsolved Murders: True Crime Stories
Hosts: Carter Roy and Wenndy Mackenzie
Frequency: Weekly
Average Show Length: 30 Minutes

Description:
Unsolved Murders: True Crime Stories is a podcast drama with a modern twist on old time radio that delves into the mystery of true cold cases and unsolved murders. With the help of an ensemble cast, follow our hosts as they take you on an entertaining journey through the crime scene, the investigation and attempt to solve the case. With many surprising plot twists, it's important you start listening from the first episode of a cold case. New episodes are released every other Tuesday. Unsolved Murders: True Crime Stories is part of the Parcast Network and is a Cutler Media Production.

Here's The Thing with Alec Baldwin
Host: Alec Baldwin
Frequency: Weekly
Average Show Length: 40 Minutes

Description:
From WNYC Studios, award-winning actor Alec Baldwin takes listeners into the lives of artists, policy makers and performers. Alec sidesteps the predictable by going inside the dressing rooms, apartments, and offices of people we want to understand better: Ira Glass, Lena Dunham, David Brooks, Roz Chast, Chris Rock and others. Hear what happens when an inveterate guest becomes a host.

Working On A Masterplan: Dating Up
Host: LaTrina McDonald
Frequency: Weekly
Average Show Length: 30 Minutes

Description:
To understand the art of dating is by loving oneself. To master dating and relationships you must understand that it is about connecting, giving, building and sometimes letting go. Once you understand these basic concepts you will know how to work on your own master plan. What is the master plan? Its you. Instead of focusing on finding the one, turn your focus to becoming the one. Working on a Masterplan is a show dedicated to an honest ongoing conversation for everything regarding dating and relationships. The difference between this show and others is that it deals with issues from the inside out. It will no doubt make you second guess what you thought you knew, forcing you to take a honest look at what you truly bring to a relationship. Its cool to know how and where to go to find a partner but what about keeping one.? The Working on a Masterplan show will guide you into finding your power, identifying your voice and creating a balance to allow you the opportunity to manifest meaningful and healthy relationships into your life. The host of Working on a Masterplan is author, host and life & dating coach LaTrina McDonald.

StoryCorps
Host: Various
Frequency: Weekly
Average Show Length: 20 Minutes

Description:
StoryCorps travels the country collecting the stories of everyday people, who get to take the microphone and interview each other about their lives. Each week, the StoryCorps podcast shares these unscripted conversations, revealing the wisdom, courage, and poetry in the words of people you might not notice walking down the street.

The Generation Why Podcast
Host: Various
Frequency: Weekly
Average Show Length: 60 Minutes

Description:
Unsolved murders, controversies, mysteries, conspiracies, & true crime.

48 Hours
Host: Various
Frequency: Weekly
Average Show Length: 40 Minutes

Description:
Experience the best in intriguing crime and justice cases that touch on all areas of the human experience, including greed and passion, presented by the award-winning team at CBS News' "48 Hours." The team's in-depth approach storytelling takes listeners inside the most difficult crime cases and human drama. For 27 seasons, "48 Hours" has developed a rich history of original reporting that has helped exonerate wrongly convicted people, caused cold cases to be reopened and solved, and along the way changed lives.

Stuff Mom Never Told You
Host: Cristen Conger and Caroline Ervin
Frequency: Weekly
Average Show Length: 60 Minutes

Description:
Hosted by Cristen Conger and Caroline Ervin, Stuff Mom Never Told You is the audio podcast from HowStuffWorks that gets down to the business of being women from every imaginable angle.

Strangers
Host: Lea Thau
Frequency: Weekly
Average Show Length: 40 Minutes

Description:
From Lea Thau, Peabody award-winning producer and creator of The Moth Podcast and The Moth Radio Hour, comes her new storytelling baby, Strangers, part of KCRW's Independent Producer Project. Each episode is an empathy shot in your arm, featuring true stories about the people we meet, the connections we make, the heartbreaks we suffer, the kindnesses we encounter, and those frightful moments when we discover that WE aren't even who we thought we were. Strangers is a proud member of Radiotopia, from PRX.

Dear Sugar
Hosts: Cheryl Strayed and Steve Almond
Frequency: Weekly
Average Show Length: 30 Minutes

Description:
The universe has good news for the lost, lonely and heartsick. Dear Sugar is here, and speaking straight into your ears. Hosted by the original Sugars, Cheryl Strayed and Steve Almond, the podcast fields all your questions — no matter how deep or dark — and offers radical empathy in return.

Call Your Girlfriend
Hosts: Ann Friedman and Aminatou Sow
Frequency: Weekly
Average Show Length: 30 Minutes

Description:
A podcast for long distance besties everywhere. Co-hosted by your new BFFs Ann Friedman and Aminatou Sow.

The Vanished Podcast
Host: Marissa Jones
Frequency: Weekly
Average Show Length: 60 Minutes

Description:
The Vanished is a true crime podcast that explores the stories of those who have gone missing. Join host, Marissa Jones, as she investigates each case, often interviewing the loved ones who are still searching for answers.

TEDTalks Society and Culture
Host: Various
Frequency: Weekly
Average Show Length: 15 Minutes

Description:
Thought-provoking videos about life and being human, with ideas from business leaders, psychologists and researchers speaking onstage at the TED conference, TEDx events and partner events around the world. You can also download these and many other videos free on TED.com, with an interactive English transcript and subtitles in up to 80 languages. TED is a nonprofit devoted to Ideas Worth Spreading.

The Dangerous History Podcast
Host: CJ
Frequency: Weekly
Average Show Length: 60 Minutes

Description:
The Dangerous History Podcast covers the history that the Establishment would rather you NOT know, helping you learn the past so you can understand the present and prepare for the future.

Stuff They Don't Want You To Know Audio
Hosts: Matt Frederick and Matt Bowlin
Frequency: Weekly
Average Show Length: 60 Minutes

Description:
From UFOs to psychic powers and government conspiracies, history is riddled with unexplained events. You can turn back now or learn the Stuff They Don't Want You To Know, an audio podcast from HowStuffWorks.com.

Unexplained
Host: Richard MacLean Smith
Frequency: Weekly
Average Show Length: 30 Minutes

Description:
Unexplained is a bi-weekly podcast about strange and mysterious real life events that continue to evade explanation. A show about the space between what we think of as real and what is not. Where the unknown and paranormal meets some of the most radical ideas in science today. When something is inexplicable, that mystery in itself can become the story. In many ways, it is often the lure of the mystery that keeps us coming back for more... And maybe, ultimately, some things are just better left unexplained.

Real Crime Profile
Hosts: Jim Clemente, Laura Richards and Lisa Zambetti
Frequency: Weekly
Average Show Length: 90 Minutes

Description:
Join Jim Clemente (former FBI profiler), Laura Richards (criminal behavioral analyst, former New Scotland Yard) and Lisa Zambetti (Casting director for

CBS' Criminal Minds) as they profile behavior from real criminal cases.

Bruce Lee Podcast
Hosts: Shannon Lee and Sharon Ann Lee
Frequency: Weekly
Average Show Length: 50 Minutes

Description:
Bruce Lee's wisdom for a harmonious life. Join Bruce Lee's daughter Shannon Lee and culture analyst Sharon Ann Lee for a conversation about the life and philosophy of Bruce Lee. Bruce Lee was a famous martial artist, movie star and cultural icon--but his philosophy has caught fire around the world inspiring millions searching for meaning and consciousness. Each episode will dig deep into Bruce's philosophy to provide guidance and action on cultivating your truest self. "Empty your mind, be formless, shapeless like water. Now you put water into a cup, it becomes the cup, you put water into a bottle, it becomes the bottle, you put it in a teapot, it becomes the teapot. Now water can flow or it can crash. Be water, my friend."

The History Chicks
Hosts: Beckett Graham and Susan Vollenweider
Frequency: Weekly
Average Show Length: 60 Minutes

Description:
Two women. Half the population. Several thousand years of history. About an hour. Go.

True Murder
Host: Dan Zupanksy
Frequency: Weekly
Average Show Length: 120 Minutes

Description:
Every week host Dan Zupansky will interview the authors that have written about the most shocking killers of all time.

Rotated Views
Host: Various
Frequency: Weekly
Average Show Length: 60 Minutes

Description:
"Presenting Life From Different Perspectives" From dealing with everyday challenges, to parenthood and everything in between; the crew breaks down life from their own point of view, delivering pure entertainment and valuable takeaways.

Another Round
Hosts: Heben and Tracy
Frequency: Weekly
Average Show Length: 60 Minutes

Description:
Heben Nigatu and Tracy Clayton cover everything from race, gender and pop culture to squirrels, mangoes, and bad jokes, all in one boozy show.

Aubrey Marcus Podcast
Host: Aubrey Marcus
Frequency: Monthly
Average Show Length: 60 Minutes

Description:
AMP is about the idea of bringing balance back into a world that is increasingly polarized, and a sense of tribe back to a people growing increasingly solipsistic. True to the concept this channel blends humor with gravity and levity with depth, as we explore the realms of the mind, psychedelics, athletics, MMA and Sexuality. Buckle up and enjoy the ride!

SPORTS & RECREATION

PARDON MY TAKE

Hosts: PFT Commenter and Dan "Big Cat" Katz

Frequency: Daily

Average Show Length: 60 Minutes

On "Pardon My Take," Big Cat & PFT Commenter deliver the loudest and most correct sports takes in the history of the spoken word. Daily topics, guests, and an inability to tell what the hosts might be doing will make this your new favorite sports talk show. This is a podcast that will without a doubt change your life for the better- guaranteed, or your money back. *Pretend a reggaeton air horn is going off right now*

The Fighter & The Kid

Hosts: Brendan Schaub and Bryan Callen
Frequency: Weekly
Average Show Length: 120 Minutes

Description:
The Fighter & The Kid is a weekly podcast featuring UFC heavyweight Brendan Schaub, and actor/comedian Bryan Callen. It's uncut and unedited and sometimes it's just ridiculous.

The Bill Simmons Podcast

Host: Bill Simmons
Frequency: Weekly
Average Show Length: 60 Minutes

Description:
HBO's Bill Simmons relaunches the most downloaded sports podcast of all-time with a rotating crew of celebrities, athletes and media members, as well as mainstays like Cousin Sal, Joe House and other friends and family members who always happen to be suspiciously available.

PTI
Hosts: Tony Kornheiser and Michael Wilbon
Frequency: Daily
Average Show Length: 20 Minutes

Description:
Tony Kornheiser and Michael Wilbon face off on the day's hottest topics.

The Herd with Colin Cowherd
Host: Colin Cowherd
Frequency: Daily
Average Show Length: 120 Minutes

Description:
The Herd with Colin Cowherd is a thought-provoking, opinionated, and topic-driven journey through the top sports stories of the day.

Sports Gambling Radio
Host: Adam Burke
Frequency: Daily
Average Show Length: 40 Minutes

Description:
BangTheBook Radio is the industry leader in presenting sports betting information and analysis. Our radio show segments feature some of the most profitable handicappers and sharpest analysts in the wagering markets of college football, NFL, MLB, NHL, NBA, college basketball, and UFC. Host Adam Burke guides the discussion through important sports gambling topics and free picks are always available on these podcasts. Whether you're just looking to build your bankroll, are new to betting on sports, or know what you're doing and want to get better, BangTheBook Radio is the place for you.

Skip and Shannon: Undisputed
Host: Adam Burke
Frequency: Daily
Average Show Length: 60 Minutes

Description:
The Skip and Shannon: Undisputed podcast. Skip Bayless, Shannon Sharpe, and Joy Taylor discuss the biggest topics of the day. It's unscripted and unfiltered.

Mike & Mike
Hosts: Mike Greenberg and Mike Golic
Frequency: Daily
Average Show Length: 60 Minutes

Description:
Mike Greenberg and Mike Golic break down the top news, games and drama throughout the sports world.

The Tony Kornheiser Show
Host: Tony Kornheiser
Frequency: Daily
Average Show Length: 60 Minutes

Description:
"The Tony Kornheiser Show" (now available exclusively on-demand) is a topical, daily talk show that starts with sports and quickly moves into politics, current events, entertainment and, really, whatever happens to be on Tony's mind that day. The format of the show—regular sit-in guests with familiar interviews and segments—highlights not only the unique perspective of Tony Kornheiser but also the expertise of his network of friends. Join one of the most recognizable and outspoken commentators of sports and entertainment (longtime radio host in Washington, DC and current co-host of ESPN's PTI) and enjoy original episodes published every weekday.

Fantasy Focus Football
Host: Matthew Berry, Field Yates and Stephania Bell
Frequency: Daily
Average Show Length: 60 Minutes

Description:
ESPN fantasy experts Matthew Berry, Field Yates and Stephania Bell provide daily strategy, previews and injury reports.

The Dan Le Batard Show
Host: Dan Le Batard
Frequency: Daily
Average Show Length: 60 Minutes

Description:
Dan Le Batard and company tackle the big issues with thought-provoking discussion.

TrueHoop
Host: Amin Elhassan
Frequency: Daily
Average Show Length: 60 Minutes

Description:
ESPN's TrueHoop team breaks down the NBA.

First Take
Hosts: Stephen A. Smith and Max Kellerman
Frequency: Daily
Average Show Length: 90 Minutes

Description:
First Take is always a heated discussion as Stephen A. Smith, Max Kellerman and guests debate about the day's top stories.

Unquestionably Raw Podcast
Hosts: Pete Toal and Mat Miller
Frequency: Daily
Average Show Length: 60 Minutes

Description:
The "Unquestionably Raw Podcast" is a multi episode per week podcast featuring NBA Basketball news, notes and analysis. Co-hosted by Pete Toal and Mat Miller, featuring many guest panelists & professional NBA experts providing insight throughout the year.

Talk Is Jericho
Host: Chris Jericho
Frequency: Weekly
Average Show Length: 90 Minutes

Description:
Recorded from all over the globe, multiple time world champion pro wrestler, lead singer of Fozzy and New York Times best-selling author Chris Jericho rocks the podcast world with "Talk Is Jericho," his unique, weekly take on all things pop culture and life in general. Sit down with Chris as he interviews some of the biggest names in entertainment and discusses the minutia of wrestling, music, television, movies and twerking!! All-ages welcome. No ID required!

The Fantasy Footballers
Hosts: Andy Holloway, Jason Moore, and Mike "The Fantasy Hitman" Wright
Frequency: Daily
Average Show Length: 60 Minutes

Description:
Fantasy Football at it's very best. Say goodbye to the talking heads of Fantasy Football and hello to The Fantasy Footballers. The expert trio of Andy Holloway, Jason Moore, and Mike "The Fantasy Hitman" Wright break down the world of Fantasy Football with astute analysis, strong opinions, and matchup-winning advice you can't get anywhere else.

Russillo & Kanell
Hosts: Ryen Russillo and Danny Kanell
Frequency: Daily
Average Show Length: 40 Minutes

Description:
Ryen Russillo and Danny Kanell bring their own flavor to the game, mixing some pop culture with the latest happenings.

The Ringer NBA Show
Host: Chris Vernon
Frequency: Weekly
Average Show Length: 50 Minutes

Description:
The Ringer's Chris Vernon hosts an NBA-centric podcast with various Ringer staffers, players, coaches, front-office personnel, insiders, and more!

The Steve Austin Show
Host: Steve Austin
Frequency: Weekly
Average Show Length: 90 Minutes

Description:
Live from Hollywood, CA by way of the Broken Skull Ranch, Pro Wrestling Hall of Famer, Action Movie/TV star, Steve Austin lets loose on these no-holds barred, explicit versions of the program. Steve gets down and dirty with Hollywood celebrities, past wrestling buddies, present pros, MMA fighters, athletes, movie stuntmen and more.

The Dan Patrick Show
Host: Dan Patrick
Frequency: Daily
Average Show Length: 40 Minutes

Description:
Listen to the Dan Patrick daily radio show. With exclusive insider access, Patrick brings A-list guests from the world of sports and entertainment to The Dan Patrick Show. Sharing his perspective on pop culture and sports, Patrick also brings a dose of humor to his fans.

Jim Rome's Daily Jungle
Host: Jim Rome
Frequency: Daily
Average Show Length: 40 Minutes

Description:
Jim Rome's Daily Jungle is a show round-up of the best of The Jim Rome Show from that particular day. The best Takes, Interviews, Calls, Soundbites, and more.

The Lowe Post
Host: Zach Lowe
Frequency: Weekly
Average Show Length: 60 Minutes

Description:
ESPN's Zach Lowe talks to various basketball people about various basketball things.

Fantasy Football Today
Host: Adam Aizer
Frequency: Weekly
Average Show Length: 60 Minutes

Description:
Want to dominate your league and get Fantasy Football bragging rights? Join host Adam Aizer and get analysis from writers Dave Richard, Jamey Eisenberg, Heath Cummings and the rest of our crew throughout the year. Start or Sit, Buy or Sell, Grade the Trade and plenty of your emails. This is the only podcast you'll need to win your league.

Something To Wrestle
Host: Bruce Prichard
Frequency: Weekly
Average Show Length: 180 Minutes

Description:
If you've always wanted to know what the real story was behind some of wrestling's biggest moments, the MLW Radio Network's Something to Wrestle with Bruce Prichard will finally give you the real answer. A terrific storyteller, Bruce has done and seen it all and now he's going to share it all with you so sit back and be ready for a wild ride! Join Bruce and his partner in crime, Conrad Thompson as they take you through the WWF's expansion in the 80s, Houston Wrestling, the challenging early 90s for the WWF, the GWF, the Monday Night War, the 2000s in WWE and TNA and so much more! Jump in Brother Love's DeLorean and go back in time as Bruce and Conrad pull back the curtain and take you inside some of wrestling's most outrageous, controversial and fascinating moments.

The Down & Dirty Radio Show
Hosts: Jim Beaver and Ami Houde
Frequency: Weekly
Average Show Length: 120 Minutes

Description:
Jim Beaver and Ami Houde bring you the #1 Off-Road and Action Motorsports Radio Show on the planet covering the world of off-road, rally, drifting, motocross & snocross with the hands down the biggest interviews in motorsports!

The Starters
Hosts: J.E. Skeets and Tas Melas
Frequency: Weekly
Average Show Length: 60 Minutes

Description:
The Starters is a daily NBA podcast hosted by J.E. Skeets and Tas Melas that breaks down the league's biggest games, storylines, and off-court antics.

Jalen & Jacoby

Hosts: Jalen Rose and David Jacoby
Frequency: Daily
Average Show Length: 60 Minutes

Description:
Jalen Rose and David Jacoby give the people what they want, breaking down sports and pop culture as only they can.

Jim Beaver's Project Action

Host: Jim Beaver
Frequency: Weekly
Average Show Length: 90 Minutes

Description:
Jim Beaver's Project Action is the place where action sports, celebrities, and badasses collide. Hosted by professional off-road racer, media personality, and nationally syndicated radio host Jim Beaver, Project Action is your weekly glimpse behind the scenes with some of the biggest personalities in the world today from Action Sports, MMA, Racing, Sports, Hollywood, and Music. Join Jim Beaver and some of his badass friends every Thursday as they take you on a ride you won't find anywhere else.

The MMA Hour

Host: Ariel Helwani
Frequency: Weekly
Average Show Length: 240 Minutes

Description:
The MMA Hour is a weekly show that features interviews with the biggest names in mixed martial arts. It is usually longer than an actual hour, and it is hosted by Ariel Helwani.

Men In Blazers

Host: Michael Davies and Michael Bennett
Frequency: Weekly
Average Show Length: 60 Minutes

Description:
We discuss football. And wear blazers. Usually at the same time. Men in Blazers is driven by the belief that Soccer is America's Sport of the Future. As it has been since 1972.

The Forward
Host: Lance Armstrong
Frequency: Weekly
Average Show Length: 60 Minutes

Description:
The Forward with Lance Armstrong gives the audience a rare and revealing listen into Armstrong's conversations with some of the most interesting people he's met through the years. Guests of the weekly podcast include an eclectic range of personalities—some well-known, others simply with intriguing stories to tell—from the world of politics, entertainment, art, business, sport and more. The podcast, which often touches on current events, is also a community forum where the audience is encouraged to send questions, comments and any feedback directly to Armstrong. Above all, The Forward Podcast is a personal, honest, engaging and always entertaining dialogue that leaves the listener with new insights and information every week.

The Right Time with Bomani Jones
Host: Bomani Jones
Frequency: Daily
Average Show Length: 40 Minutes

Description:
Bomani Jones shares his unique thoughts on the biggest stories in sports and beyond.

Peter King, The MMQB Podcast
Host: Peter King
Frequency: Weekly
Average Show Length: 60 Minutes

Description:
"The MMQB Podcast with Peter King" is the ultimate destination for all things pro football. Led by one of the most influential storytellers in all of sports media, three-time American Sportswriter of the Year Peter King, "The MMQB Podcast with Peter King" is an access-driven experience that brings fans into the locker room, the press box and the front office with the biggest influencers in professional football. Fans can listen in on in-depth conversations with the biggest names in football that they haven't heard before to get a fresh, new and intimate experience on America's most popular sport.

UFC Unfiltered
Hosts: Jim Norton and Matt Serra
Frequency: Weekly
Average Show Length: 90 Minutes

Description:
UFC Unfiltered with Jim Norton and Matt Serra" is the must-listen podcast for fight fans. Edgy veteran comedian Jim Norton and former UFC welterweight champion Matt Serra push the boundaries in the UFC's first audio series. "Unfiltered" delivers everything, including pre- and post-fight analysis, industry stories, observations, opinions and interviews with UFC sources, fighters and celebrity fans.

The Vertical Podcast
Host: Adrian Wojnarowski
Frequency: Weekly
Average Show Length: 60 Minutes

Description:
Adrian Wojnarowski, the most dominant force in NBA reporting, brings you inside the league with, the "Vertical Podcast." Woj is probing the biggest newsmakers in the sport – from the commissioner, to general managers, coaches and star players – to bring listeners inside the processes, personas and stories that impact the NBA. Beyond longer sit-down interviews in our New York studios, Woj will deliver real-time podcasts with league personnel built around breaking news.

Ringer University
Hosts: Mallory Rubin, Chris Vernon and Ben Glicksman
Frequency: Weekly
Average Show Length: 60 Minutes

Description:
The Ringer's podcast universe joins the collegiate ranks with Ringer University, a feed dedicated to what's happening in college football and beyond, with in-house talents Mallory Rubin, Chris Vernon, and Ben Glicksman serving up insights, picks, and predictions on a week-to-week basis throughout the season.

Around the NFL
Hosts: Gregg Rosenthal, Dan Hanzus, Marc Sessler and Chris Wesseling
Frequency: Weekly
Average Show Length: 60 Minutes

Description:
NFL.com's "Around the NFL" crew (Gregg Rosenthal, Dan Hanzus, Marc Sessler and Chris Wesseling) break down the latest football news, with a dash of mirth.

NBA Lockdown
Host: Various
Frequency: Weekly
Average Show Length: 60 Minutes

Description:
NBA Lockdown covers all of the latest news, rumors and opinions with ESPN's team of experts.

The Dirtbag Diaries
Host: Fitz Cahall
Frequency: Weekly
Average Show Length: 30 Minutes

Description:
This is adventure. Climbing. Skiing. Hiking. Biking. Travel. Whatever your passion, we are all dirtbags. Outdoor writer Fitz Cahall and his team presents stories about the dreamers, athletes and wanderers.

Art of Wrestling
Host: Colt Cabana
Frequency: Weekly
Average Show Length: 60 Minutes

Description:
Colt Cabana continues to wrestle ALL OVER THE WORLD. Each week he sits down, in person, with a friend in wrestling to tell their stories of struggle and triumph in an attempt to live their dream. Episodes also include rare music, hilarious stories, commentaries and more.

The Ross Report
Host: Jim Ross
Frequency: Weekly
Average Show Length: 90 Minutes

Description:
WWE Hall of Famer Jim Ross, considered the greatest announcer in wrestling history, brings his incredible celebrity roster of friends, his insight and analysis of today's wrestling stars and storylines, and YOU to his weekly discussion of everything squared circle. Join in the fun as Good Ol' JR takes your calls, makes a few of his own, and spreads the wrestling love around the globe.

The Ringer NFL Show
Host: Robert Mays, Kevin Clark, Mallory Rubin and Tate Frazier
Frequency: Weekly
Average Show Length: 50 Minutes

Description:
The Ringer NFL Show will be hosted by a rotating group of The Ringer NFL experts including Robert Mays, Kevin Clark, Mallory Rubin, and Tate Frazier, the show will also feature surprises guests including ex-players and coaches.

Outside Podcast
Hosts: Brian Ardinger, Matt Boyd and Paul Jarrett
Frequency: Weekly
Average Show Length: 50 Minutes

Description:
Brought to you by the editors of Outside, this podcast aims to apply the magazine's long-standing literary storytelling methods to the audio realm. Each episode is either prompted by a feature from the archives or simply inspired by a theme Outside has explored. The podcast's first series delves into the science of survival in some of nature's most extreme environments. Presented by PRX and Outside magazine.

The Ric Flair Show
Host: Ric Flair
Frequency: Weekly
Average Show Length: 90 Minutes

Description:
The MLW Radio Network presents The Ric Flair Show. Join the 16 time World Heavyweight Champion "The Nature Boy" Ric Flair® and Conrad Thompson as they talk about the "good ole days" with their friends like Hulk Hogan, "Stone Cold" Steve Austin, Sting, Bret "Hitman" Hart, Mick Foley, Terry Funk, Kurt Angle, Eric Bischoff, and every other major name in wrestling from the last 40 years. On occasion, Ric will have some of his other friends on the show too like NFL Hall of Famer Lawrence Taylor and even Grammy Award Winning Darius Rucker.

Bischoff on Wrestling
Host: Eric Bischoff
Frequency: Weekly
Average Show Length: 90 Minutes

Description:
The MLW Radio Network presents Bischoff on Wrestling! With over twenty-five years in sports entertainment, Eric Bischoff brings a fresh take on the topics fans are most passionate about. Whether it's a main event from the most recent episode of RAW, fallout from a big WWE Network special, major news & rumors on the backstage politics of sports entertainment, or the rapidly emerging Indy wrestling scene: nothing is off limits. Catch "Bischoff on Wrestling," every Wednesday, exclusively from PodcastArena. com!

TECHNOLOGY

2017 Technology Top Pick
TED RADIO HOUR
Host: Guy Raz
Frequency: Weekly
Average Show Length:
50 Minutes

The TED Radio Hour is a journey through fascinating ideas: astonishing inventions, fresh approaches to old problems, new ways to think and create. Based on Talks given by riveting speakers on the world-renowned TED stage, each show is centered on a common theme – such as the source of happiness, crowd-sourcing innovation, power shifts, or inexplicable connections. The TED Radio Hour is hosted by Guy Raz, and is a co-production of NPR & TED.

Reply All
Hosts: PJ Vogt and Alex Goldman
Frequency: Weekly
Average Show Length: 40 Minutes

Description:
A show about the internet. And trained rats, time travel, celebrity dogs, lovelorn phone scammers, angry flower children, workplace iguanas, and more. Hosted by PJ Vogt and Alex Goldman, from Gimlet.

Note To Self
Host: Manoush Zomorodi
Frequency: Weekly
Average Show Length: 40 Minutes

Description:
Is your phone watching you? Can wexting make you smarter? Are your kids real? These and other essential quandaries facing anyone trying to preserve their humanity in the digital age. Join host Manoush Zomorodi for your weekly reminder to question everything.

TEDTalks Technology
Host: Various
Frequency: Weekly
Average Show Length: 10 Minutes

Description:
Some of the world's leading inventors and researchers share demos, breakthroughs and visions onstage at the TED conference, TEDx events and partner events around the world. You can also download these and many other videos free on TED.com, with an interactive English transcript and subtitles in up to 80 languages. TED is a nonprofit devoted to Ideas Worth Spreading.

Decrypted
Host: Brad Stone
Frequency: Weekly
Average Show Length: 30 Minutes

Description:
The global technology industry is a powerful engine of innovation that drives the economy. It's also a collection of insular communities full of hidden projects, quiet rivalries, and uncomfortable truths. Join Bloomberg Technology's Brad Stone each week as he and the team's reporters uncover what actually happens behind closed doors.

WSJ Tech News Briefing
Host: Various
Frequency: Daily
Average Show Length: 5 Minutes

Description:
Stay informed on the latest technology trends with daily insights on what's hot and happening in the world of technology. Listen to our WSJD reporters discuss notable tech company news, new tech gadgets, personal technology updates, app features, start-up highlights and more.

This Week in Tech
Host: Leo Laporte
Frequency: Weekly
Average Show Length: 120 Minutes

Description:
Your first podcast of the week is the last word in tech. Join the top tech

pundits in a roundtable discussion of the latest trends in high tech.

The Jay & Farhad Show
Host: Jay Yarow and Farhad Manjoo
Frequency: Weekly
Average Show Length: 30 Minutes

Description:
A technology podcast starring Jay Yarow, executive editor for CNBC, and Farhad Manjoo, columnist for The New York Times. Produced by Matt Edwards.

TechStuff
Host: Jonathan Strickland
Frequency: Weekly
Average Show Length: 60 Minutes

Description:
TechStuff is a show about technology. And it's not just how technology works. Join host Jonathan Strickland as he explores the people behind the tech, the companies that market it and how technology affects our lives and culture.

The Tech Guy
Host: Leo Laporte
Frequency: Weekly
Average Show Length: 120 Minutes

Description:
No one does a better job of explaining technology, computers, and the Internet than Leo Laporte. This feed contains the full audio of his twice weekly radio talk show as heard on stations all over the US on the Premiere Radio Networks. For show notes and more visit techguylabs.com.

a16z
Host: Andreessen Horowitz
Frequency: Weekly
Average Show Length: 30 Minutes

Description:
The a16z Podcast discusses tech and culture trends, news, and the future -- especially as 'software eats the world'. It features industry experts, business leaders, and other interesting thinkers and voices from around the world. This podcast is produced by Andreessen Horowitz (aka "a16z"), a Silicon Valley-based venture capital firm.

Security Now
Host: Steve Gibson
Frequency: Weekly
Average Show Length: 120 Minutes

Description:
Steve Gibson, the man who coined the term spyware and created the first anti-spyware program, creator of Spinrite and ShieldsUP, discusses the hot topics in security today with Leo Laporte.

Still Untitled: The Adam Savage Project
Host: Adam Savage
Frequency: Weekly
Average Show Length: 30 Minutes

Description:
Posted on Tuesdays, Norm and Will discuss topics of interest with Adam-- nothing is off-limits! Still Untitled covers everything from hot-button issues within the maker community to experiences from Adam's life to questions from the audience. Enjoy!

Learn to Code With Me
Host: Laurence Bradford
Frequency: Weekly
Average Show Length: 30 Minutes

Description:
The Learn to Code With Me podcast, created by Laurence Bradford, is for aspiring techies and self-taught coders looking to transition into the tech industry. Want actionable insights on how you can get paid for your coding skills? Then you're in the right place!

Software Engineering Daily
Host: Jeff Meyerson
Frequency: Weekly
Average Show Length: 60 Minutes

Description:
Technical interviews about software topics.

Design Details
Hosts: Bryn Jackson and Brian Lovin
Frequency: Weekly
Average Show Length: 60 Minutes

Description:
A show about the people who design our favorite products. Hosted by Bryn Jackson and Brian Lovin.

Exponent
Hosts: Ben Thompson and James Allworth
Frequency: Weekly
Average Show Length: 60 Minutes

Description:
Exponent, a production of Stratechery.com, is hosted by Ben Thompson and James Allworth. In this program we seek to explore the massive effect technology is having not just only technology companies, but also on society as a whole. Ben Thompson is the author of Stratechery, a blog about the business and strategy of technology. James Allworth is the co-author with Clay Christensen of "How Will You Measure Your Life" and a writer for the Harvard Business Review.

Software Engineering Radio
Host: Various
Frequency: Weekly
Average Show Length: 60 Minutes

Description:
Software Engineering Radio is a podcast targeted at the professional software developer. The goal is to be a lasting educational resource, not a newscast. Every 10 days, a new episode is published that covers all topics software engineering. Episodes are either tutorials on a specific topic, or an interview with a well-known character from the software engineering world.

Recode Decode
Host: Kara Swisher
Frequency: Weekly
Average Show Length: 60 Minutes

Description:
One of tech's most prominent journalists, Kara Swisher is known for her insightful reporting and straight-shooting style. Listen in as she hosts hard-hitting interviews about the week in tech with influential business leaders and outspoken personalities from media, politics and more.

Programming Throwdown
Host: Patrick Wheeler and Jason Gauci
Frequency: Weekly
Average Show Length: 60 Minutes

Description:
Programming Throwdown attempt to educate Computer Scientists and Software Engineers on a cavalcade of programming and tech topics. Every show will cover a new programming language, so listeners will be able to speak intelligently about any programming language.

Cortex
Host: CGP Grey and Myke Hurley
Frequency: Weekly
Average Show Length: 90 Minutes

Description:
CGP Grey and Myke Hurley are both independent content creators. Each episode, they discuss the methods and tools they employ to be productive and creative. Hosted by CGP Grey and Myke Hurley.

Talking Machines
Hosts: Katherine Gorman and Ryan Adams
Frequency: Weekly
Average Show Length: 40 Minutes

Description:
Talking Machines is your window into the world of machine learning. Your hosts, Katherine Gorman and Ryan Adams, bring you clear conversations with experts in the field, insightful discussions of industry news, and useful answers to your questions. Machine learning is changing the questions we can ask of the world around us, here we explore how to ask the best

questions and what to do with the answers.

Coding Blocks
Hosts: Allen Underwood, Michael Outlaw and Joe Zack
Frequency: Weekly
Average Show Length: 120 Minutes

Description:
The world of computer programming is vast in scope. There are literally thousands of topics to cover and no one person could ever reach them all. One of the goals of the Coding Blocks podcast is to introduce a number of these topics to the audience so they can learn during their commute or while cutting the grass. We will cover topics such as best programming practices, design patterns, coding for performance, object oriented coding, database design and implementation, tips, tricks and a whole lot of other things. You'll be exposed to broad areas of information as well as deep dives into the guts of a programming language. While C# and Microsoft. NET are our preferred development platform, most topics discussed are relevant in any number of Object Oriented programming languages such as Java, Ruby, PHP, etc.. We are all web and database programmers so we discuss Javascript, HTML, SQL and a full spectrum of technologies and are open to any suggestions anyone might have for a topic.

Linear Digressions
Hosts: Ben Jaffe and Katie Malone
Frequency: Weekly
Average Show Length: 20 Minutes

Description:
In each episode, your hosts explore machine learning and data science through interesting (and often very unusual) applications.

MacBreak Weekly
Host: Leo Laporte
Frequency: Weekly
Average Show Length: 120 Minutes

Description:
Get the latest Apple news and views from the top names in Mac, iPhone, iPod, and iPad journalism.

Vergecast
Hosts: Nilay Patel and Dieter Bohn
Frequency: Weekly
Average Show Length: 90 Minutes

Description:
The Vergecast is your source for an irreverent and informative look at what's happening right now (and next) in the world of technology and gadgets. Hosted by Nilay Patel and Dieter Bohn, alongside a cavalcade of tech luminaries, Vergecast is the only podcast you need to make sense of the week in tech news. And your life.

Partially Derivative
Hosts: Jonathan Morgan, Vidya Spandana and Chris Alban
Frequency: Weekly
Average Show Length: 40 Minutes

Description:
The everyday data of the world around us, hosted by data science super geeks. For the nerdy and nerd curious.

Accidental Tech Podcast
Hosts: Marco Arment, Casey Liss and John Siracusa
Frequency: Weekly
Average Show Length: 120 Minutes

Description:
Three nerds discussing tech, Apple, programming, and loosely related matters.

The CyberWire
Host: David Bittner
Frequency: Daily
Average Show Length: 15 Minutes

Description:
The CyberWire Daily Podcast is our look at what's happening in cyberspace. We provide a clear and concise summary of the news and offer commentary from industry experts as well as our Academic and Research Partners. Each Friday, we provide the usual daily summary along with a look back at the news for the entire week.

Marketplace Tech
Host: Ben Brock Johnson
Frequency: Daily
Average Show Length: 5 Minutes

Description:
Marketplace Tech®, hosted by Ben Brock Johnson, tackles the business behind the technology that's obsessing us and changing our lives. With the listener in mind, this weekday segment examines everything from video games and robots to consumer protection and space travel. Marketplace Tech is part of the Marketplace® portfolio of public radio programs broadcasting nationwide, which additionally includes Marketplace, Marketplace Morning Report®, and Marketplace Weekend®. Listen on-air each weekday or online anytime at marketplace.org. From American Public Media.

Defensive Security Podcast
Hosts: Jerry Bell and Andrew Kalat
Frequency: Daily
Average Show Length: 60 Minutes

Description:
Defensive Security is a weekly information security podcast which reviews recent high profile security breaches, data breaches, malware infections and intrusions to identify lessons that we can learn and apply to the organizations we protect.

No So Standard Deviations
Hosts: Roger Peng and Hilary Parker
Frequency: Weekly
Average Show Length: 60 Minutes

Description:
Not So Standard Deviations: The Data Science Podcast Roger Peng and Hilary Parker talk about the latest in data science and data analysis in academia and industry. Co-hosts: Roger Peng of the Johns Hopkins Bloomberg School of Public Health and Hilary Parker of Stitch Fix.

Windows Weekly
Hosts: Paul Thurrott and Mary Jo Foley
Frequency: Weekly
Average Show Length: 90 Minutes

Description:
A weekly look at all things Microsoft, including Windows, Windows Phone, Office, Xbox, and more, from two of the foremost Windows watchers in the world, Paul Thurrott of Thurrott.com and Mary Jo Foley of All About Microsoft.

Tech News Today
Hosts: Megan Morrone and Jason Howell
Frequency: Weekly
Average Show Length: 40 Minutes

Description:
Tech News Today explores the most important stories of the day in conversation with the world's leading journalists.

Back To Work
Hosts: Merlin Mann and Dan Benjamin
Frequency: Weekly
Average Show Length: 90 Minutes

Description:
Back to Work is an award winning talk show with Merlin Mann and Dan Benjamin discussing productivity, communication, work, barriers, constraints, tools, and more. Hosted by Merlin Mann & Dan Benjamin.

Ctrl-Walt-Delete
Hosts: Merlin Mann and Dan Benjamin
Frequency: Weekly
Average Show Length: 60 Minutes

Description:
Back to Work is an award winning talk show with Merlin Mann and Dan Benjamin discussing productivity, communication, work, barriers, constraints, tools, and more. Hosted by Merlin Mann & Dan Benjamin.

The Energy Gang
Hosts: Jigar Shah, Katherine Hamilton and Stephen Lacey
Frequency: Weekly
Average Show Length: 60 Minutes

Description:
The Energy Gang is an energy digest produced by Greentech Media. The show features engaging discussion between energy futurist Jigar Shah, energy policy expert Katherine Hamilton and Greentech Editor Stephen Lacey. Join us as we delve into the technological, political and market forces driving energy and environmental issues.

Apple Keynotes
Host: Tim Cook
Frequency: Quarterly
Average Show Length: 120 Minutes

Description:
The Apple Keynotes podcast offers video of the company's most important announcements, including presentations by Apple CEO Tim Cook.

WANT TO START YOUR OWN PODCAST?

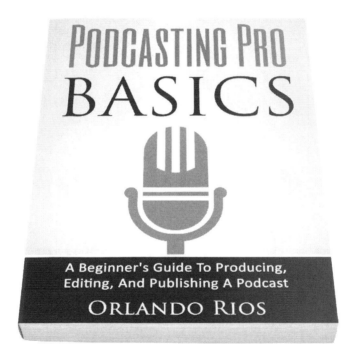

Download Podcasting Pro Basics FREE at
PodcastingPro.com/freebook

Printed in Great Britain
by Amazon